· CONCISE GUIDE TO ·

Navicular Syndrome in the Horse

Also by David W. Ramey, D.V. M.

Horsefeathers: Facts Versus Myths About Your Horse's Health

Concise Guide to Medications and Supplements for the Horse

Concise Guide to Tendon and Ligament Injuries in the Horse

Concise Guide to Colic in the Horse

· CONCISE GUIDE TO ·

Navicular Syndrome in the Horse

David W. Ramey, D.V.M.

Howell Book House
New York

Howell Book House
A Simon & Schuster Macmillan Company
1633 Broadway
New York, NY 10019

MACMILLAN is a registered trademark of Macmillan, Inc.

Library of Congress Cataloging-in-Publication Data

Ramey, David W.
    Concise guide to navicular syndrome in the horse / David W. Ramey.
        p. cm.
    Includes bibliographical references and index.
    ISBN 0-87605-913-2
        I. Navicular diseases.   I. Title.
    SF959.N39R35   1997   96-8496
    636.1'0897398—dc20   CIP

Manufactured in the United States of America

10 9 8 7 6 5 4 3 2 1

CONTENTS

Contents

ACKNOWLEDGMENTS

As with the other books in this series, I am delighted to be able to express a sincere debt of gratitude for the helpful suggestions and comments of a number of people. My secretary, Denise (Leeper) Steele was invaluable in reviewing the manuscript. Linda Rarey, intrepid crime fighter, found time for reading and reviewing in her busy schedule yet again and helped to make the book cogent. The fine illustrations were once again provided by Lynda Fenneman, loyal client, illustrator extraordinaire and the proud owner of Zamora the wonder horse. Finally, to my best friend and confidante, Elizabeth, thanks for all your help, suggestions and encouragement. Glad you've signed on for the duration.

INTRODUCTION

Navicular syndrome. Most likely no condition of the horse's limbs is as feared by horse owners as is navicular syndrome. Probably no condition is as frequently suspected as a cause of lameness in the horse as disease of the horse's navicular bone. Certainly, few conditions that cause lameness in the horse are as frequently diagnosed as is navicular syndrome.

In the author's opinion, much of this fuss is unwarranted. While navicular syndrome is certainly a serious condition that causes lameness in the horse, it is also a condition that is frequently over-diagnosed. It is the "first diagnosis of the diagnostically destitute," according to one authority. Navicular syndrome in the horse is a serious condition that requires a thoughtful approach to diagnosis. Treatment of this condition can be frustrating. However, it is not the first condition that should be immediately considered when any horse shows lameness.

This book was written in an attempt to help clear up many of the concerns and misconceptions about navicular syndrome in the horse. It will help show you what the condition is, and explain some of the current thoughts as to how the condition develops. The book will discuss the diagnosis and treatment of the condition. It will show you why disease of the navicular bone is normally not an easy diagnosis to make.

Hopefully, it will also help you understand why it is a diagnosis that is often easily made, even if that diagnosis isn't warranted.

With the information that you will gain from this book, you should be able to help participate in the detection of the cause of your horse's lameness. Should he be diagnosed as having navicular syndrome, with the help of the book you should be able to help select and understand a treatment. Finally, you should be able to make some realistic decisions about your horse's future based on what you learn here.

Navicular syndrome is not what you probably think. Like any problem, it is one that needs to be approached with thoughtfulness and understanding, in a rational way. With the help of this book, you can approach your horse's lameness, a problem that you will be unquestionably concerned with, in such a manner.

CHAPTER I

Some Normal Anatomy and Physiology of the Horse's Foot As It Relates to Navicular Syndrome

Frankly, anatomy can be pretty boring stuff. However, before you can begin to understand what navicular syndrome in the horse is (and is not), you have to understand what and where the navicular bone is. Familiarizing yourself with the complex anatomy of the horse's foot is essential to understanding the problem of navicular syndrome. What follows is not a complete anatomic description of the foot; that would be too time-consuming, technical and tedious for this book. Instead, most of the important features of this area that pertain to the navicular bone have been highlighted. There is enough basic anatomy and physiology information here so that you can ultimately begin to figure out this problematic condition of the horse's foot (and hopefully not so much as to make you crazy).

THE BONES, TENDONS AND LIGAMENTS OF THE HORSE'S HOOF

The Bones of the Foot

Bone is the framework upon which the horse's body is built. Happily, there are only three bones that make up the framework of the horse's foot.

The only bone that is really obvious on a standing horse is called the second phalanx by anatomists (everyone else calls it the short pastern bone). Even though it helps make up the framework of the foot, most of the second phalanx is not contained inside the hoof. However, the lower surface of this bone makes up part of the joint of the foot. The bone itself also serves as the attachment for some very important ligaments.

Below the pastern bone (towards the ground) and contained within the hoof itself is the second of the three bones, known as the third or distal phalanx (known to horse people as the "coffin" bone). The coffin bone meets with the short pastern bone above and helps form the joint of the foot. The coffin bone has a rather unique shape. As you might suspect, the leading edge of the bone is shaped in an arc, just like the horse's hoof. But if you cut through the hoof parallel to the ground and looked down from the top, you'd see that the entire coffin bone is shaped sort of like a quarter moon.

Lying just above and within the curve of the quarter moon is the distal sesamoid bone, commonly known as the navicular bone (the source of your concern). The word "navicular" comes from the Latin word for boat. Perhaps, when you look at the bone from one direction on an X ray, you can imagine the keel of a boat. (See figure 4 in chapter 4.)

· Figure I ·

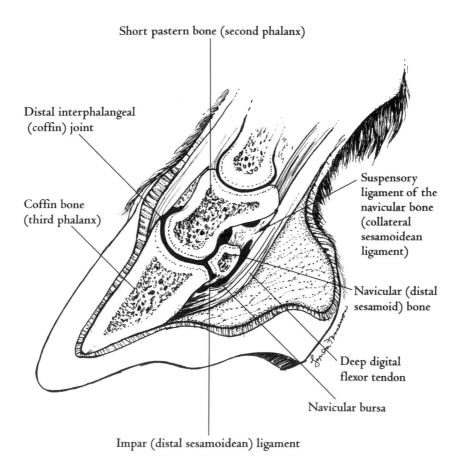

Short pastern bone (second phalanx)

Distal interphalangeal
(coffin) joint

Coffin bone
(third phalanx)

Suspensory
ligament of the
navicular bone
(collateral
sesamoidean
ligament)

Navicular (distal
sesamoid) bone

Deep digital
flexor tendon

Navicular bursa

Impar (distal sesamoidean) ligament

Cross-section of foot as seen from the side.

The Joint of the Foot

Any point in the horse's body where two bones meet is called a joint. The ends of the bones that meet in joints are covered with a unique substance called cartilage. Cartilage provides a smooth, almost frictionless gliding surface for the bones to move against each other. It also helps cushion the ends of the bones when they are squeezed together by the weight of the horse. Inside the joint, a fluid (synovial fluid) is produced to provide nutrition to the cartilage cells and to help lubricate the joint. This fluid is produced by the lining cells of the joint capsule, which surrounds the joint. The joint capsule is the wrapping paper that keeps the package that is the whole joint together.

The joint of the foot (the "coffin" joint) is made of contacting surfaces of all three of the bones of the foot (see figure I). The surfaces of all these bones are intimately associated with each other. Thus, the fluid in the coffin joint is in contact with some surface of all three of the bones at some point.

Because they are so intimately associated with each other, it can sometimes be extremely difficult (even impossible) for someone (like your veterinarian) to precisely distinguish between the various bones and joint surfaces when there is a problem in the horse's heel or foot area. The joint fluid that touches one area touches them all. This has some important implications for the diagnosis of problems in this area, as you will see in later chapters.

Of particular interest to people who are interested in navicular syndrome (of which you, presumably, are one) is the structure of the joint around the navicular bone. The navicular bone normally has little depressions and surface irregularities in it where it contacts the lining of the coffin joint. The coffin joint lining can even make little indentations into the navicular bone. These fossae (as the depressions are called) can frequently be seen on X rays. There is a great deal of discussion in the veterinary community about the significance of these fossae in relation to navicular syndrome (much more on them later).

The Ligaments of the Foot

Ligaments are supporting structures that, in the case of the foot (as well as in most other areas), connect bone to bone. Ligaments are stabilizing straps of connective tissue. Their function is to try to keep the bones in a constant relationship to each other. (If you placed two boxes next to each other and taped the sides so that the boxes would stay together, the tape would be serving the same function for the boxes as ligaments do for bone.) For example, there are collateral ligaments of the foot that run along both sides of the coffin and short pastern bones. Of much more interest (at least in regard to how ligaments pertain to navicular syndrome) are two other ligaments that attach to the navicular bone (see figure 2).

The collateral sesamoidean ligaments (commonly called the suspensory ligaments of the navicular bone) begin from little depressions on either side of the large first phalanx (also known as the long pastern bone; it's immediately above the second phalanx). One ligament curves around and behind each side of the short pastern bone (second phalanx) and attaches to each end, as well as to the top side of the navicular bone. Branches of these ligaments also attach to the coffin bone. These suspensory ligaments effectively suspend the navicular bone in its spot, tucked in behind the coffin bone and below the short pastern bone.

The distal sesamoidean ligament (the impar ligament) ties the bottom of the navicular bone down to the coffin bone. It's a short little ligament that begins at the bottom (distal) border of the navicular bone and ties into the coffin bone on its ground side, just under where the large deep flexor tendon inserts into the coffin bone.

· FIGURE 2 ·

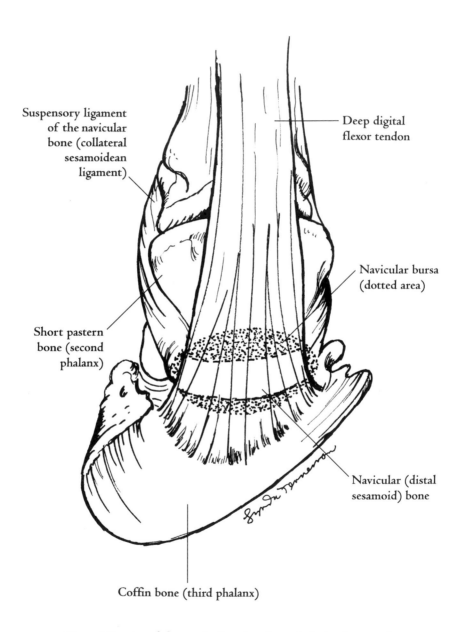

Suspensory ligament
of the navicular
bone (collateral
sesamoidean
ligament)

Deep digital
flexor tendon

Navicular bursa
(dotted area)

Short pastern
bone (second
phalanx)

Navicular (distal
sesamoid) bone

Coffin bone (third phalanx)

View of foot from below and off to the side, with the hoof removed.

The Deep Flexor Tendon

Tendons connect muscles to bone. When a muscle contracts (contracting is the only thing a muscle can do) it causes the bone to move via the tendon. The tendon transmits the force of the contracting muscle to the bone. (Of course, tendons have many other important functions. That is the sort of stuff found in *Concise Guide to Tendon and Ligament Injuries in the Horse.*)

Of concern to the whole problem of navicular syndrome is a large, important tendon that runs down the back of the horse's leg. This is the tendon of the deep digital flexor muscle (commonly called the deep digital flexor tendon).

The deep flexor tendon begins at the level of the horse's knee (carpus) and descends down the back of the lower limb (or digit; hence the term "digital"). It can easily be felt down in the area behind the horse's cannon bone as well as lower, behind the pastern. It runs down underneath the heel and directly over the top of the navicular bone. It then inserts into the coffin bone (and over the top of the impar ligament of the navicular bone).

The Navicular Bursa

Between the deep digital flexor tendon and the navicular bone lies a bursa. A bursa is a fluid-filled sac that is found in various locations in the horse's body. Bursae occur anywhere a tendon makes a turn over the top of a bone. For example, there's an important bursa in your shoulder where the tendons make the turn down your arm. A bursa is like a little pillow that helps to cushion the turn of the tendon. The navicular bursa in the horse helps to cushion the deep flexor tendon as it makes its turn over the top of the navicular bone.

The navicular bursa is implicated by some veterinarians as the source of many of the problems that are involved with navicular syndrome. Its actual role in navicular syndrome is still being investigated. (There's more on this subject later.)

The Nerve Supply to the Navicular Bone

The nerves that give sensation to the navicular area are a subject of great interest to those who study navicular syndrome. It's vitally important to know which nerves of the navicular bone area go to what part. There are two main reasons for this (besides just plain curiosity).

The first reason is for diagnostic purposes. As you will learn, one of the common diagnostic techniques used for determining whether or not a horse has navicular syndrome (or indeed, any type of lameness) is the nerve block. In this technique, local anesthetic is placed over the nerves that go to an area; alternatively, anesthetic may be injected directly into a joint. If the horse is limping because a particular area hurts and the area that hurts is made numb, presto, the horse will stop limping. You can then assume that the numb area is where the pain that caused the limp came from.

Obviously, to do the best job that you can at interpreting this sort of procedure, it helps to know precisely where the nerves that you are "blocking" go. Conversely, if you're not sure where the nerves go, you can't make a very accurate determination as to what the problem is. (This, by the way, is just one of the problems in making an accurate diagnosis of navicular syndrome.)

The second reason for knowing about the nerves of the navicular area is surgical. In horses that do not respond to any treatment for navicular syndrome, occasionally a surgical neurectomy (cutting the nerves) is recommended. Obviously, you have to know where the nerves are to find them, cut them and understand what effect this is going to have on the horse.

There are two major nerves that travel down to the navicular bone. These paired nerves are called the palmar digital nerves ("palmar" refers to the posterior aspect of the front leg). They arise at the level of the horse's fetlock joint and descend down the back of the horse's pastern. The nerves lie just to the side of the large deep digital flexor tendon and in close association with the major veins and arteries of the back of the foot (see figure 3). Importantly, these large nerves do not only supply the navicular bone. They also provide sensation to the entire heel area of the horse's foot. Importantly, by blocking the sensation in these nerves with local anesthetic, you remove the sensation to the whole heel area, not just the navicular bone. This has important implications for the proper diagnosis of navicular syndrome.

At the level of the navicular bone itself, the nerve supply becomes quite complex. Most of the nerves that supply the navicular bone itself travel through the impar ligament and the collateral sesamoidean ligaments. The inner surface of these ligaments also makes up part of the lining for the joint of the foot (the coffin joint). This has important implications for the interpretation of local anesthetic blocks of the coffin joint, as you will see in chapter 4.

The nerve supply to the navicular bursa goes along a slightly different path. The nerves to the navicular bursa also travel through the impar and collateral sesamoidean ligaments, but on the opposite side (the ground side) from the nerves that go to the navicular bone itself. Although the nerves that travel through this area mostly supply the navicular bursa, they also provide sensation to a small part of the surface of the deep flexor tendon where it runs over the bursa. It's also possible to put anesthetic into this area as part of a diagnostic work-up for navicular syndrome.

· FIGURE 3 ·

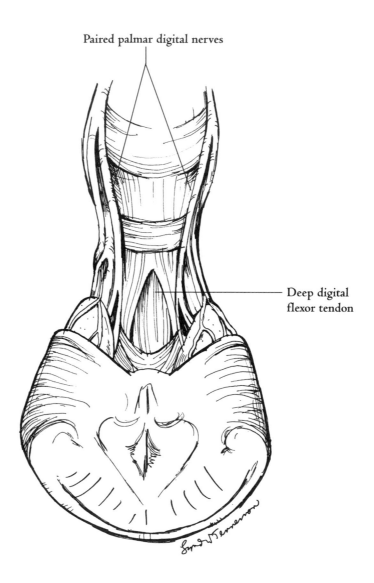

Paired palmar digital nerves

Deep digital
flexor tendon

From behind the pastern, with the skin and superficial tissues removed, the palmar digital nerves can be seen. Note the deep flexor tendon running down the center of the pastern.

HOW THE FOOT MOVES

The coffin joint is what anatomists call a "hinge" joint (actually, the term is ginglymus joint, but that's not exactly a conversational term). That is to say that when the joint moves, it opens and closes like the hinge on a door. It's the same type of movement that you have in your elbow, although in the joint of the horse's foot, obviously, there's a lot less movement than in your elbow.

The coffin joint is extended (pulled up and forward) by a large extensor tendon that attaches to the top and front of the coffin bone. It is flexed (pulled up and bent back) by the action of the tendon of the deep digital flexor muscle. The flexion action is made easier by the navicular bone.

The deep digital flexor tendon makes a bend around the navicular bone (a bend that is cushioned by the navicular bursa). This turn in the tendon apparently allows the navicular bone to act like the fulcrum in a lever system. (If you use a bar to pry a rock up out of the ground, your work is made a lot easier if you put a piece of wood under the end of the bar to pry up against. That piece of wood is called the fulcrum.) Just like the fulcrum in a lever system, the navicular bone is an important stress point for the horse's entire foot.

When the horse's foot strikes the ground, in the majority of horses that have been studied the heel (the back part of the foot) strikes the ground first. (In the rest of the horses studied, the foot lands flat.) The rest of the foot follows the heel onto the ground in sequence, from the back of the foot to the front. The weight of the horse causes the hoof to be compressed and to spread out as it is mashed into the ground.

As the foot continues to bear weight, the structures of the foot are pushed downward into the ground. The force from the horse's weight is pushed straight down to the ground and passes directly through the navicular bone, the navicular bursa, the flexor tendon and the digital cushion of the foot. (The digital cushion is like a pillow that sits between all the sensitive structures inside the foot and the hard tissue that contacts the ground.) To accommodate the pressure, the foot expands. The expansion of the foot directs the forces to the outer margins of the foot. The forces then travel up and out the hoof wall. (Some additional shock absorption is provided by the blood in the horse's foot. The blood in the foot acts like a fluid-filled pillow. Following the principle of hydraulics, the blood in the foot also helps to get rid of the stress that is applied to the foot by the horse's weight.)

When the full weight of the horse is on the foot and the structures of the foot have sunk as low as they can, the deep flexor muscle acts. It pulls on the bottom of the coffin bone (and over the top of the navicular bone). This causes an initial downward pull on the horse's toe as the whole foot begins to be pulled back and up. As the horse continues to travel forward, his leg rolls over the toe of the foot and the whole foot structure comes up off the ground. The foot then travels through the air as the horse strides forward. Finally, the foot will hit the ground and begin the whole cycle all over again.

The back part of the horse's foot (the heel) thus comes under a lot of stress in the course of a normal stride. The horse's heels are a very sensitive area. They are the shortest part of the foot and the closest to the ground. Because they are shorter, they are also softer than any other part of the foot. They normally hit the ground first. Finally, research shows that they take a greater part of the force at impact on the ground than any other part of the foot. It's no wonder (and it's a fact) that this short, soft, stressed area of the horse's foot is the area that is most commonly affected by lameness!

Because the heels are so frequently involved as a cause of lameness in the horse and because there are so many structures that lie in the heel area, it's extremely important for you to remember one thing: *Not all lameness that originates in the horse's heels is associated with the navicular bone!* Injury to any one of the structures in the heels, including the digital cushion, the impar ligament, the suspensory ligaments of the navicular bone, the navicular bursa, the coffin joint, the coffin bone or the navicular bone itself (among others) can be associated with lameness. Depending on your definition, any of these structures may be associated with navicular syndrome, too. (For the author's definition, read on.)

CHAPTER 2

Navicular Syndrome Defined

WHEN YOU ARE TRYING TO COME UP WITH A CONCISE definition for navicular syndrome, right away you get into trouble. Believe it or not, there is no generally accepted definition of the term "navicular syndrome" in the veterinary community. More than anything else, this reflects the fact that navicular syndrome is a complex and poorly understood condition. If it were easy to understand, it would be easy to define (and easy to recognize and probably easier to treat).

As a matter of fact, there's not even general agreement to call the condition navicular syndrome. Many people refer to the problems that occur in and around the horse's navicular bone as navicular disease.

What's the difference? Well, in some ways it's a matter of semantics. But it's really more than that. Disease is, by definition, "A definite morbid process having a characteristic train of symptoms" (*Dorland's Illustrated Medical Dictionary*, 25th Edition, W. B. Saunders Co., Philadelphia, 1974). Thus, to call problems associated in and around the horse's navicular bone a "disease" is to imply that the condition has a regular and recognizable set of factors that occur with it. When you think of a "disease," you think of a well-wrapped package of clinical signs, diagnostic elements and treatments.

With abnormalities in and around the navicular bone, however, you have anything but a neat package of events. Therefore, in the minds of many veterinarians (the author included), the use of the term "disease" to describe what's going on in and around the horse's navicular bone isn't appropriate. A better term to describe the condition is "syndrome."

A syndrome is, by definition, "A set of symptoms which occur together" (*Dorland's*, op. cit.). It's a much more general term than "disease." By calling the problems that occur in and around the horse's navicular bone a "syndrome," veterinarians acknowledge that they don't know exactly what's going on. The use of the word "syndrome" implies that you are dealing with a complex condition, one that may have many potential treatments.

Of course, once you've decided to call it something, then you have to decide what that something is. With navicular syndrome, that's the hard part. Navicular syndrome may actually involve a complex of diseases and injuries that affect the heel area of the horse's foot. The reasons that these diseases and injuries occur are poorly understood. There may be many factors involved. In its broadest terms, navicular syndrome may involve a number of structures, including (among other structures) the navicular bone, the navicular bursa, the blood supply to the area, the joint of the foot (the coffin joint), the suspending ligaments of the navicular bone and the deep digital flexor tendon.

However, some veterinarians prefer a more narrow definition for the term navicular syndrome. They feel that the term specifically refers to a condition that only involves the horse's navicular bone and one of the other associated structures. For example, these veterinarians feel that a navicular ligament problem is completely different from a problem involving the navicular bone. They think the two conditions should be considered separately. And, in many ways, they're right. The prognosis for recovery from a ligament injury is most likely completely different from that of a problem involving degeneration of the navicular bone itself. The challenge for veterinary medicine (and veterinarians), then, is in trying to distinguish between the various things that can cause soreness in the heel area of the horse, the area where the navicular bone lies. So far, that's not something veterinary medicine can do very well.

What does the author of this book think? The philosophy of this book is that a more narrow definition of the term navicular syndrome is appropriate. That is, the use of the term navicular syndrome should be confined to those horses in which disease of the navicular bone itself can be reasonably suggested. Otherwise, even broader terms, such as heel soreness or caudal foot soreness, can be used to describe horses that have poorly defined lameness originating from the back part of the foot. To the author, the term "navicular syndrome" implies a chronic, incurable condition associated with deterioration of the navicular bone. When appropriate, by using the term "heel soreness" instead of "navicular syndrome," the author attempts to distinguish between those horses that have an incurable condition (long-term deterioration of the navicular bone) and those horses that may be able to recover from their problems. In fact, given the large number of structures involved and the complex anatomy in the horse's heel, the odds are that a particular horse with pain in the heels does not have pain specifically coming from the navicular bone. In the author's mind, calling all horses with heel pain of undetermined cause "navicular" is painting them all with a very broad and damning brush. In the author's experience, most horses with deep heel pain of undetermined cause get better; most horses with navicular syndrome do not.

Granted, all this is probably a bit confusing to you. Unfortunately, it almost has to be. At this point in time, it's confusing to everyone. The development, diagnosis and treatment of navicular syndrome isn't well understood by anyone. There isn't even a consensus in the veterinary community about what the syndrome is. Navicular syndrome is not a nice, neat package. Therefore, it is predictable that you will hear all sorts of opinions about navicular syndrome in the horse. Conflicting, sometimes almost opposing, statements can be heard from individuals who are well educated and well respected in the veterinary field. At this time, there is no single right solution to the problem of navicular syndrome.

Thus, in a way, even the title of this book is a bit of an oxymoron. There is no concise box into which navicular syndrome can be fit. However, it is possible to understand what navicular syndrome is and what it is not. It is possible to make some rational treatment decisions for your horse if he has been properly diagnosed with navicular syndrome. You can make some reasonable predictions about what is going to happen to horses that are affected with the condition. The following chapters should help you do just that.

CHAPTER 3

Navicular Syndrome: Pathology and Theories of Development

A NUMBER OF THEORIES HAVE BEEN DEVELOPED AS TO the underlying cause of navicular syndrome. They're not really all that technical and they can be interesting. It is somewhat important for veterinarians to try to figure out why the problem occurs. After all, if you could get to the root cause of navicular syndrome, then you could make some reasonable recommendations for treatment.

Unfortunately (at least for those of you who like easy answers), when it comes to navicular syndrome, the word "multifactorial" comes to mind. That means there may not be a single cause of the problem. That also means, of course, that there may be no single solution, either. Some part of each of the many theories of development of navicular syndrome may contribute to the condition itself.

ISCHEMIC THEORY

Ischemia is defined as a loss or lack of blood supply to an area. In 1979, it was proposed that navicular syndrome in the horse was caused by problems in the circulation of blood to the navicular bone. This theory proposed that, in horses with navicular syndrome, little blood clots formed in the small arteries running to the navicular bone. These clots would block the normal circulation of blood to the bone. As a result, there would be pain resulting from the loss of circulation and bone death in the area supplied by the little arteries that were plugged up by the clots. (It would resemble what happens in the process of heart disease in people.)

If, as a result of the proposed ischemia, bone began to die (which would be the normal response to the loss of circulation), the horse's body would have to remove the dying bone. This could then leave a navicular bone with little holes in it from where dead bone was removed. That might explain the typical X-ray changes that are seen in the bones of horses with navicular syndrome (more on that later).

Unfortunately, at least insofar as support for this theory goes, nobody has been able to show that this theoretical situation is what actually happens. When navicular bones from horses that have had navicular syndrome are looked at under the microscope, nobody has been able to find any blood clots in the little arteries, or areas of bone dying from a lack of circulation.

If this ischemic theory were true, at least some part of effective treatment would logically be aimed at affecting the horse's circulation. However, as you will see, even though the ischemic theory of navicular syndrome can't be supported based on the scientific evidence, some component of navicular syndrome may involve the circulation of blood in or to the bone. In fact, some treatment to affect the circulation to the horse's foot is a commonly traveled avenue of therapy for navicular syndrome.

MECHANICAL THEORIES

Mechanical theories for the development of navicular syndrome suggest that the condition develops due to physical stress on the horse's foot, particularly in the heel area. That is, due to some combination of poorly defined factors, there are abnormal stresses applied to the horse's foot. These stresses result in changes to the navicular bone. Interestingly, from a therapeutic standpoint, the mechanical theories suggest that if you can improve the way that the horse's foot moves, you may be able to help relieve the stress on the foot and thereby treat the condition.

Most people don't realize that bone is active, living tissue. Like most other tissues in the horse's body, it is constantly replacing itself as cells wear out. Because it is living and continually changing, bone also responds to stress. When pressure (stress) is applied to bone, the bone responds by increasing its activity (this is called remodelling). Stressed bone removes old and adds new bone at a more rapid pace than would normally occur. Stressed areas of bone generally also become thicker over time. Changes in the navicular bone that occur as a result of stress may be part of the problem that begins the navicular syndrome. Actually, all or parts of any of the following theories may have something to do with the development of the problem.

Increased Bone Activity Theory

In 1982 in Denmark, a theory was developed which proposed that horses with navicular syndrome had bone that was more active than normal bone. This increased bone activity was theorized to be a result of increased pressure on the navicular bone. This pressure was said to be applied by the deep digital flexor tendon where it travels over the top of the bone. (In fact, the area where the navicular bone is in contact with the deep flexor tendon is the area where most of the observed abnormalities of the diseased navicular bone occur.) With this theory, anything causing an increased stress on the back of the foot, such as poor foot conformation, for example, could start a horse down the road to navicular syndrome.

Interestingly, this theory of navicular syndrome also suggests that the condition is reversible if it is caught early enough. That is, if the stresses on the navicular bone can be recognized and corrected early enough, it should be possible for the bone to go back to its pre-stressed normal state. Only after secondary changes in and around the navicular bone occur (as a result of long-term deterioration of the bone) would a horse with navicular syndrome be considered incurable.

Navicular Bursitis Theory

The navicular bursitis theory, proposed over thirty years ago, states that the navicular bursa is the culprit. As you remember, the navicular bursa is a little fluid-filled sac that lies between the deep flexor tendon and the navicular bone. It cushions the deep flexor tendon as it turns around the bone. Anyway, if the navicular bursa became inflamed due to repeated concussion and stress, a process of inflammation could begin that might even extend into the navicular bone and surrounding structures.

Bursitis (inflammation of a bursa) is a condition that exists in many different species; for example, in the human shoulder. Recent studies have suggested that the navicular bursa may, in fact, become inflamed in some horses. Local anti-inflammatory injections into the navicular bursa have been tried as a form of therapy (more on that in later chapters). However, navicular bursitis certainly does not seem to be a major contributor to the development of the navicular syndrome in the horses that have been studied so far.

Vibrational Theory

In the vibrational theory, proposed in 1969, the deep flexor tendon phys-ically breaks down the navicular bone. That is, due to poor conformation (or some other contributing factor), microvibrations of the deep flexor tendon cause friction between the two surfaces (like friction generated by rubbing your hands together). Over time, this friction grinds away at the surface of the navicular bone, causing erosion of the bone and deterioration of the opposing surface of the tendon that touches the bone. It's an interesting idea but one that really hasn't received any serious study.

DEGENERATIVE THEORY

The degenerative theory is supported by research out of Norway. It says that navicular syndrome is a process similar to what occurs in the breakdown of joints (degenerative joint disease). In fact, the changes that are seen in the diseased bone of horses with navicular syndrome do look something like the changes that are seen in bone that comes from diseased joints. Of course, nobody knows why joints break down and become arthritic either, so while the theory is very interesting, it's not particularly helpful in understanding what is actually happening in navicular syndrome. Still, some forms of therapy are directed at treating navicular syndrome as an arthritis-like condition, with some reported success.

UNIFIED THEORY

In 1989, veterinarians at the University of California-Davis proposed a theory for the development of navicular syndrome that incorporated elements of all of the above theories. Key elements of their theory include:

1. The underlying disease process is one of degeneration and deterioration of the bone, similar to what is seen in arthritis of the horse's pastern (ringbone) or hock (bone spavin).

2. The changes are caused by abnormal mechanical forces on the foot and navicular bone. Importantly, from a therapeutic standpoint, these forces may be altered.

3. These mechanical forces cause the navicular bone to begin to change. Some horses may successfully make changes to their navicular bones to adapt to the stress, and never show any signs of lameness. Some horses may show occasional lameness until the bone changes its structure to accommodate the stress. However, the navicular bones of other horses may ultimately not be able to cope with the stress. These are the horses that will eventually have chronic changes in the navicular bone and become permanently lame. (Unfortunately, however, at this time there is no way to tell any of these horses apart.) At some point in the disease process, the clinical features of all these horses may be identical.

4. As chronic changes occur in the structure of the navicular bone, the system of blood drainage from the bone may be adversely affected. Blood drainage may become sluggish. This poor drainage of blood causes an increased pressure inside the navicular bone. The increase in bone pressure causes the pain demonstrated by the horse.

This theory does seem to tie together a lot of the scientific knowledge that has been gained about navicular syndrome over the years. It suggests that navicular syndrome is a process that occurs over time. It suggests that some horses can recover from the condition if their disease process is recognized in time and the mechanical stresses on the foot are somehow altered or allowed to subside. It explains why drugs that affect the horse's circulation may be useful in treatment of the condition. Unfortunately, it also suggests that after permanent changes in the navicular bone have occurred, it may never be possible to return the horse to normal function.

Perhaps now you have some understanding of the complex nature of the theories of development of navicular syndrome. As you can see, navicular syndrome isn't a cut-and-dried problem. But you should be able to see where therapy for horses with navicular syndrome will be directed. Treatment will be made in efforts to change the mechanical forces on the foot, to control pain and inflammation, to affect the circulation to the foot and to control the deterioration of the bone. (All the information on how veterinarians and farriers try to do this is contained in the chapters that follow.) But first, you'll want to know the steps that veterinarians take to make a diagnosis of navicular syndrome. Read on!

CHAPTER 4

The Diagnosis of Navicular Syndrome

WHEN A HORSE LIMPS, HE IS SAID TO BE LAME. Navicular syndrome is a cause of lameness, usually front leg lameness, in the horse. A horse that is affected with navicular syndrome is always lame. Although this seems rather obvious, it's also very important. People overlook this simple fact. It will save you a lot of grief if you remember two simple things about navicular syndrome:

1. A horse that shows no signs of clinical lameness, that is, a horse that is not limping or shows no signs of abnormal movement, cannot be said or determined to be suffering from navicular syndrome under any circumstances.

2. You cannot predict whether any horse is going to develop navicular syndrome using any method of diagnosis.

That being said, there are some important factors that have been associated with the development of navicular syndrome in individual horses. Certain diagnostic tests are used to help make a diagnosis of the condition. Most, if not all, of these tests need to be used in order to properly establish a diagnosis of navicular syndrome. However, *no single test can be used to diagnose navicular syndrome in the horse.*

The proper diagnosis of navicular syndrome in the horse is not easy. For example, it cannot be done just by looking at the horse's foot. Nor can it be diagnosed merely by observing the way a particular horse travels (even if he is lame). Thus, the statement "Gee, your horse is lame. I wonder if he has a touch of navicular?" is merely rash and irresponsible. Such a statement reflects ignorance on the part of the person saying it. (So don't say it.) Proper diagnosis requires careful, detailed evaluation of the horse and his lameness history.

In fact, it can sometimes be quite difficult to distinguish between navicular syndrome and other causes of heel soreness in the horse. Although it is relatively easy for a veterinarian to localize the source of a horse's lameness to his heels, it may be a real diagnostic challenge to further pinpoint the source of the lameness to a specific structure within the heel area. For example, veterinary science is unable to distinguish between a problem that might affect one of the ligaments of the navicular bone and a problem involving the bone itself. Or, it may not be possible to distinguish between a horse with heel pain coming from the digital cushion and pain coming from the deep flexor tendon in the foot.

How you choose to make a diagnosis all goes back to your definition of navicular syndrome. If you are a veterinarian and you choose to lump any cause of soreness in the horse's heels together as part of navicular syndrome, then you are going to make that diagnosis in a lot of horses. If, on the other hand, you are more restrictive in your diagnosis and you limit the use of the term navicular syndrome to only those problems that truly involve degeneration of the navicular bone, you'll probably use that diagnosis much less often and with a lot more reluctance. Either way, it's not an easy process.

FACTORS THAT MAY PREDISPOSE A HORSE TO NAVICULAR SYNDROME

Age

Contrary to what a lot of people think, navicular syndrome is generally considered to be a condition affecting younger horses. The condition is most commonly diagnosed in horses that are between seven and fourteen years of age. Horses that are less than three years old or more than fifteen years old appear to be three to five times less likely to develop navicular syndrome.

Sex

There appears to be no association with the development of navicular syndrome and the sex of the horse.

Breed

It does seem that certain breeds of horses are more frequently affected with navicular syndrome. Thoroughbreds, Quarter Horses and warmbloods seem to have a higher frequency of navicular syndrome than do other breeds. No one knows why this is so. However, navicular syndrome is also most commonly seen in athletic horses. Horses of the aforementioned breeds are those most commonly used for strenuous athletic competitions such as jumping, barrel racing and eventing. Events such as these cause considerable stress on the horse's limbs. Therefore, it's possible that what on the surface appears to be a breed predisposition for the development of navicular syndrome may only reflect the activity for which the horse is used.

Genetics

According to most authorities, navicular syndrome does not appear to be a condition that horses inherit from their parents. That is, it is believed that horses that have navicular syndrome don't tend to make more horses with navicular syndrome. However, there has been one study that suggests that the condition may be inherited. In addition, a study released in October 1995 suggests that the shape of a horse's navicular bone may be influenced by genetics (although the shape of the navicular bone has not been associated with the development of navicular syndrome).

Hoof Abnormalities

It's commonly thought that if the horse's foot isn't normal, he'll be more likely to develop navicular syndrome. A normal foot should be of the proper length, angle and balance for that individual horse.

Many types of abnormal feet have been described in the horse. What all these hoof factors have in common is that theoretically they may concentrate abnormal stresses in the horse's foot. These abnormal stresses may be particularly concentrated in the back part (the heels) where the navicular bone is located. The mechanical theories of the development of navicular syndrome suggest that abnormal stresses on the horse's foot may have something to do with causing navicular syndrome in the horse. Even if it doesn't cause navicular syndrome, an abnormal hoof is certainly not a desirable thing in any horse and it can lead to chronic hoof soreness.

Proper hoof care is extremely important in any horse. It is especially so in the horse affected with navicular syndrome. There is a great deal of information about dealing with these hoof problems and caring for the foot of the horse with navicular syndrome in chapter 6.

Conformation Abnormalities

Another thing that has been suggested as predisposing a horse to navicular syndrome is the horse's conformation. Conformation is the study of how the horse "should" be put together (as opposed to how he is actually put together). In reality, conformation is not something that you can do anything about.

Anyway, in addition to the previously mentioned foot abnormalities, many people consider a horse with upright (in relation to the ground) pasterns as being predisposed to navicular syndrome. Theoretically, an upright pastern does not bend and absorb stress as well as a more "normal" pastern. The stress has to go somewhere, however, and the navicular bone supposedly gets more than its share of stress in these horses. Similarly, some people blame small feet for predisposing a horse to navicular syndrome. There aren't any studies to support these ideas, however.

NAVICULAR SYNDROME: MAKING THE DIAGNOSIS
Lameness History

Navicular syndrome is usually an insidious thing. It often sort of sneaks up on the horse. Sometimes horses with navicular syndrome do become acutely and suddenly lame. However, it's much more common for people to notice one of a number of little things in their horse that have gotten a bit worse over time.

Perhaps you will have noticed that the horse with navicular syndrome has been traveling a bit "short" on his front legs. That is, he doesn't seem to want to reach out and land on his heels in a normal fashion. Maybe his gait seems choppy. Since the navicular bone is in the heel area of the foot, if the horse can shorten his stride he presumably won't have to land so hard on his heels. Maybe a shorter stride doesn't hurt him so much. You may have noticed that this reduction in the length of the stride has gotten worse over time.

(Curiously, when many people see a horse short-striding, they immediately think of a problem in the horse's shoulder. Although a sore shoulder muscle will cause a horse to short-stride because he doesn't want to stretch that area forward, shoulder problems in the horse are actually pretty uncommon. Most lameness problems in the horse originate from the front foot. It's a better guess if you think of a foot problem when you see a horse that doesn't want to reach forward.)

Perhaps you've seen that the horse's lameness has been intermittent. That is, he seems a bit lame on some days but just fine on others. Usually, if a horse has navicular syndrome, over time the lameness will progress and eventually become a constant problem for the horse.

Perhaps the horse's lameness gets worse with exercise (although this would be expected with most conditions that cause lameness). Conversely, he may get much better with rest. You most likely won't be able to see any obvious reason for this lameness, such as swelling or pain to manipulation of the leg, that would give you a clue as to why this might be the case.

Perhaps you've observed that the horse's lameness is worse when he is turning in a circle. When a horse makes a tight circle, more of his weight is forced over the leg on the inside of the circle. If a horse has a sore foot, as occurs with navicular syndrome, the increase in weight caused by the horse turning may cause him to show characteristic signs of lameness, such as flinching or bobbing his head when the affected leg hits the ground. Most horses that are affected with navicular syndrome seem to have the problem in both front feet. Therefore, it's not at all uncommon to see the horse limping on whichever front leg is on the inside of a tight circle.

In fact, a circle may be the only place where the lameness in a horse that has navicular syndrome is evident. When he travels in a straight line, you may not even notice that he is limping. If both feet hurt, the poor lame horse may not even know which leg to limp on! (Think of yourself walking barefoot across a hot concrete driveway. Which foot hurts the most? Can your friends tell by looking?)

Perhaps the lameness gets worse when the horse is worked on hard or rough ground. Softer ground provides more cushion to the horse's foot. Harder ground would presumably make traveling on a foot that is sore as a result of navicular syndrome more uncomfortable.

Hoof Testers

A hoof testers is a simple device and something that no equine veterinarian can be without. It's used to squeeze the horse's hoof. If the horse jumps or tries to pull his leg away when pressure is applied to his hoof with the hoof testers, it may indicate that the horse's foot is sore in the area that was squeezed. (There is a bit of an art to this, however. Some horses will jump at any pressure applied to their foot.)

A horse with navicular syndrome may react to pressure placed in certain directions with the hoof testers. Typically, horses with navicular syndrome will react to hoof testers pressure in one or all of three ways:

1. Pressure placed from the central groove (the central sulcus) of the frog to the toe.
2. Pressure placed from one of the grooves on the side of the frog (the collateral sulci of the frog) to the hoof wall on the opposite side of the groove.
3. Pressure placed across the back of the heels.

If a horse reacts to hoof testers pressure in one or more of these areas, the reaction should be consistent, repeatable and uniform before you start considering that the response is significant and that the horse may have a problem in the area. In addition, all of the other areas of the horse's foot should be checked to make sure that they aren't painful, either. After all, the response to the hoof testers that you observed in the heels could actually be originating from some other spot. Of course, you also want to make sure that the horse isn't just reacting to *any* sort of pressure on his foot.

Unfortunately, not all horses that have navicular syndrome react to hoof testers pressure. Even if a horse doesn't respond to a hoof testers, he can still have navicular syndrome. Remember, no single test can be used to make a diagnosis of this difficult condition.

Hyperextension Test

The hyperextension test is one of several types of stress test that can be performed in the diagnosis of navicular syndrome. In this test, the horse's foot is placed on one end of a board. The other side of the board is then lifted up in the air gradually. As a result, the horse's toe is levered up into the air.

This test theoretically should stretch out the structures on the back of the leg as the toe is lifted into the air. It should thus increase the tension in the deep flexor tendon and the suspensory ligament of the navicular bone. If these areas are sore, the horse may demonstrate a positive response by jumping off the board or by limping more when he is trotted off (of course, since they aren't always the most cooperative beasts, some horses are going to jump off the board when it is elevated anyway). Although a positive response to this test is interesting, a negative response does not rule out a diagnosis of navicular syndrome.

Frog Pressure Test

In the frog pressure test, a piece of wood, a stick or even a hoof knife is placed under the back two-thirds of the frog of the horse's foot. The opposite leg is then held up in the air for a minute or so, forcing the horse to stand on the chunk of wood.

Standing on an object in this manner should put pressure directly onto the structures above, including the navicular bone, navicular bursa and deep flexor tendon. If, after the opposite leg is released, the lameness in the leg that was on the object increases when the horse is trotted off, it suggests some deep heel soreness. Again, like the hyperextension test, a negative response to this test does not rule out the presence of navicular syndrome.

Flexion Test

A flexion test is commonly performed to assist in lameness diagnosis of many conditions of the horse's legs. In the front leg, a flexion test is performed by holding the fetlock joint up in the air with a moderate degree of pressure for sixty seconds or so. Immediately after the leg is released, the horse is trotted off in a straight line. Sometimes lameness, if it existed, is made worse by this test.

The flexion test makes some horses with navicular syndrome quite lame. This is most likely because the test causes some sort of compression on the structures in the back part of the horse's pastern and foot. In navicular syndrome, some or all of these structures may be sore. Compressing them apparently makes them hurt more.

Remember, when you flex the horse's fetlock joint, you not only bend that one joint, you also bend all the other joints of the lower limb. In addition, you compress all the tendons and ligaments that run down the back of the horse's leg. You may also adversely affect the flow of blood to the horse's leg when you hold it up in firm flexion. It should therefore be rather obvious that the flexion test is not a precise test for the diagnosis of navicular syndrome (in fact, it's not a precise test for much of anything). Sometimes horses that are clinically normal and have no signs of any disease will limp after a flexion test! Still, a positive response to a forelimb flexion test gives you one more bit of information when you are trying to determine whether or not a horse has navicular syndrome.

ANESTHETIC "BLOCKS"

When any lame horse is evaluated, one of the most common methods used by veterinarians to determine the source of the lameness is through the use of local anesthetic. When a horse limps, it's because he hurts somewhere. If you can remove the source of the pain, even temporarily, the horse will immediately stop limping. Thus, the use of local anesthetic "blocks" that temporarily deaden areas of the horse's leg are extremely useful in helping to determine the area from which the soreness that is making your horse limp originates.

The whole process of making a diagnosis of navicular syndrome would be made much easier if veterinarians knew exactly what structures were made numb by the various nerve blocks that are used. However, which nerves actually supply the navicular bone and its various associated structures is something that is just being figured out. In trying to make the diagnosis of navicular syndrome, three different nerve blocks may be employed. It's apparent that each of the nerve blocks will anesthetize a slightly different area. Each block will give a veterinarian a slightly different bit of information. (Prior to reading on about nerve blocks, it may be useful to review the information about the nerve supply to the navicular bone in chapter I.)

Importantly, the areas of the foot made numb by the various different anesthetic blocks overlap each other. Therefore, after one anesthetic nerve block has been performed, you may have to wait for it to wear off before you can do another block. As a result, the horse that is suspected of having navicular syndrome may have to be evaluated over a period of time, to allow for each block to wear off before starting on the next one. Like most everything else about the navicular syndrome, interpreting the anesthetic blocks is complicated.

Predictably, given the complexity of the condition, no one block is diagnostic for the navicular syndrome. It's quite a mess. (In fact, in reading the explanations of the nerve blocks that follow, it may help to have a pencil and paper in hand so that you can help keep the effects of the various blocks straight!)

Heel (Palmar Digital Nerve) Block

It's relatively easy to put a small amount of anesthetic over each of the nerves that run down the back of the horse's pastern. Thus, this is undoubtedly the most frequently performed nerve block in the horse. This procedure is the so-called palmar digital nerve block. A horse that is suffering from navicular syndrome should improve at least 90 percent from his lameness after this block. Most horses with navicular syndrome have the condition in both front feet and it's not at all uncommon for the observed lameness to switch legs after the heels of one leg are made numb with anesthetic. Since, after the block, the horse no longer feels pain in the one leg that hurts, he may begin to limp on his other leg, (the one that is now more sore). In fact, the lameness exam may be the first time you even noticed that he was sore in his other leg!

If you take only one thing from this book, this next sentence might be it. Any horse with pain in his heels, from whatever the cause, should improve with a palmar digital nerve block. A horse cannot be said to have navicular syndrome based solely on the response to this block. This block will remove the sensation from all of the structures in the horse's heel, not just the navicular bone.

Coffin (Distal Interphalangeal) Joint Block

When anesthetic is placed into the joint of the horse's foot (the coffin joint), it makes the structures in direct contact with the joint, as well as the joint itself, numb. Thus, the suspensory ligaments of the navicular bone and the impar ligament, as well as the nerve fibers that are carried in these ligaments (that run directly to the navicular bone) are likely to be anesthetized by this block. Other structures in the horse's heel, *including the navicular bursa and the deep digital flexor tendon,* are less likely to be affected by a coffin joint block (the nerves that travel to those structures are not in intimate contact with the coffin joint). Thus a coffin joint block is thought to be one way to block pain coming directly from the navicular bone and its supporting ligaments (although it appears less likely to block pain coming from some of the other structures associated with the navicular bone). However, and this is important, this block cannot distinguish between navicular bone pain and pain coming from the coffin joint itself (some horses do have foot pain as a result of arthritis of the joint).

After observing the results of a block of the coffin joint, a heel block would be a logical next step in helping to reach a lameness diagnosis. By using the blocks in combination you could assume:

1. If the horse is better after the coffin joint block but doesn't improve with a heel block, the problem is most likely to be in the coffin joint itself.

2. If the horse is better after the coffin joint block and also improves with the heel block, the problem is deep in the heel and may involve the navicular bone or its supporting structures.

3. If the horse isn't any better after the coffin joint block and improves after a heel block, the problem is in the heel but it may not involve the navicular bone (although it could involve some of the other structures associated with the navicular bone such as the navicular bursa and deep digital flexor tendon; please read on about the navicular bursa block).

4. If the horse doesn't get better after either of the blocks, the problem is somewhere else!

Navicular Bursa Block

It is possible to place anesthetic directly into the navicular bursa that lies between the deep flexor tendon and the navicular bone. If done properly, it appears that this block can provide some additional useful information in the diagnosis of navicular syndrome.

Honestly, though, this is not a block that is without potential problems. Since the navicular bursa is deep within the foot, the injection involves a bit of technical skill and some horses don't like it very much. Furthermore, it's very hard to know that you are actually in the navicular bursa with your needle, even when the needle is viewed directly with a fluoroscope! (A fluoroscope is an X-ray camera that lets you look inside the foot while you are sticking a needle in it.) In addition, complications, such as severe lameness (that sometimes does not resolve), have been reported as a result of this block. Thus, some veterinarians are reluctant to use this anesthetic block.

If the block is performed properly, it numbs the navicular bursa and the surfaces of the navicular bone and the deep digital flexor tendon (these structures make up the sides of the navicular bursa). This block can also cause a loss of feeling in the navicular bone itself if the

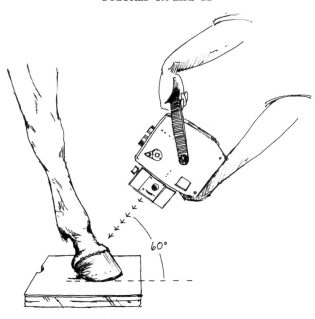

The 60-degree dorsopalmar (D-P) radiograph is taken in the manner shown here.

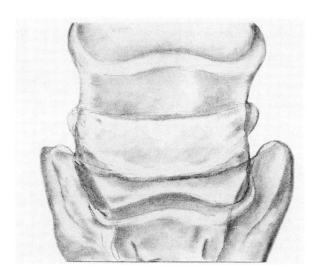

The resulting radiograph of a normal navicular bone is shown as well.

anesthetic is absorbed into the bone (say, for example, if the bone is thin due to deterioration caused by the disease process).

If it is done properly, the navicular bursa block may provide some additional specific information that cannot be obtained by using one of the other diagnostic nerve blocks. For example, horses have been seen that respond positively to a palmar digital block (of the heel) and do not respond to a coffin joint block. When the navicular bursa of these horses is blocked, the horses travel sound. This combination of results suggests a problem involving deterioration of the deep digital flexor tendon deep in the foot, for example.

Radiographs

Radiographs (X rays) are probably the most commonly used diagnostic technique for the evaluation of navicular syndrome in the horse. Portable X-ray machines are easy to use and commonly employed in lameness and prepurchase evaluations. But, oh, are radiographs of the navicular bone a source of controversy in the veterinary community!

It's easy to take X rays of the navicular bone. Usually two views of the bone are taken during a routine exam. The first view, the 60-degree dorsopalmar shot, is taken with the horse standing on the X-ray plate (figures 4a and 4b).

The angle of the X-ray beam in this technique is approximately 60 degrees to the plate. In this shot, the navicular bone is viewed through the second phalanx (short pastern bone). The second view, the "skyline" shot, is also taken with the horse on the X-ray plate but it's taken from the back of the leg, with the X-ray beam being directed down the leg and between the heels. After exposing the X-ray film in this fashion, the radiographs are then developed and evaluated for "changes" from normal. (See figures 5a and 5b.)

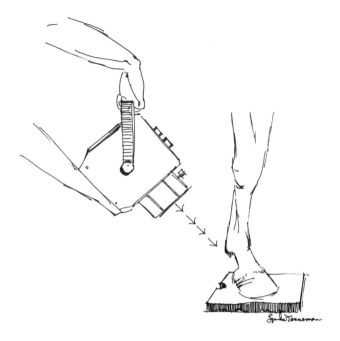

The "skyline" radiograph of the navicular bone is taken as shown here.

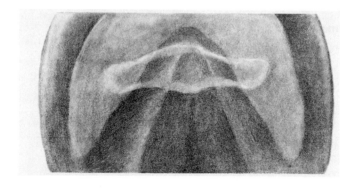

This projection results in a very different view of the navicular bone (as illustrated).

The interpretation of X rays is a bit of an art. It requires a lot of time, training and experience. It's not easy to do. Although they are most likely good people in their own right, your horse trainer, farrier or best friend are not the people who should be looking at your horse's X rays. That's the job of your veterinarian.

Everyone seems to be able to agree pretty well on what an unchanged navicular bone looks like on an X ray. However, differences of opinion arise as to what constitutes an abnormal navicular bone radiograph. Traditionally, veterinarians are trained to look for changes in the navicular bone such as little holes (some people call them lollipops), bone spurs from the edges of the navicular bone, loss of bone density and so on. Indeed, some horses that suffer from navicular syndrome do have such changes. The problem is, at least insofar as interpreting radiographs goes, so do a lot of normal horses (figure 6).

It's been well demonstrated that a variety of radiographic changes can exist in normal horses. Many of these "changes" are the normal areas along the navicular bone where the lining of the coffin joint molds into depressions of the bone (these are called synovial invaginations by veterinarians; see chapter 1). A 1992 study of 583 horses in Germany documented numerous changes in the navicular bones of horses that showed no signs of lameness. Many of these changes would be almost automatically be identified as abnormal by most veterinarians. Studies done in England have also confirmed that there is a wide variation of radiographic appearance of the navicular bone in clinically normal horses.

A study done in the United States a few years ago is really disturbing if you'd like to hang your hat on the significance of X rays of the navicular bone. In this study, thirty-five horses that had been diagnosed as being lame from navicular syndrome and fifteen normal horses were X-rayed. Of the lame horses, 70 percent had changes in their X rays. Unfortunately (from a diagnostic standpoint), so did 60 percent of the

· FIGURE 6 ·

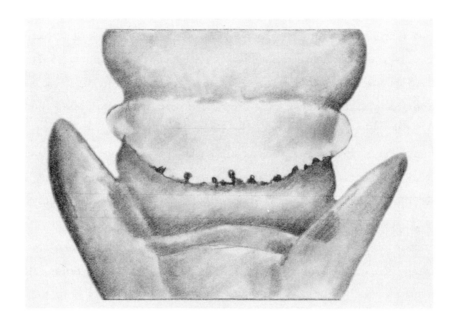

A 60-degree D-P radiograph of the navicular bone, showing changes along the lower border of the bone. Changes such as these may be completely normal for a horse. Horses with problems in the navicular bone area may also have similar changes. However, some people would wrongly consider changes such as these a definite indication of a problem in the navicular bone area whether the horse is lame or not.

normal horses! Furthermore, the veterinarians who participated in the study were not able to distinguish between horses that were lame and normal horses based solely upon their X rays.

What has become increasingly apparent is that navicular syndrome is not a condition that can be diagnosed just by using X rays. Certainly, in a horse that has all the clinical signs of navicular syndrome, X rays can be used to help confirm the diagnosis. But many clinically normal horses have bad X rays. Conversely, some horses that have navicular syndrome have no X-ray changes at all. So although X rays are an important part of the diagnostic process for navicular syndrome, they must be interpreted with care and caution. *X rays alone can never be used to make a diagnosis of navicular syndrome.* It should also be rather obvious, given the wide variety of changes that can be seen in the normal horse, that X rays can never be used to tell if a horse is going to develop navicular syndrome at some point in the future (see chapter 9).

Scintigraphy

Nuclear scintigraphy is a relatively new diagnostic technique for the examination of lame horses. Although the technique is readily available in most areas where there are a lot of horses, the equipment involved is quite expensive. Additionally, since scintigraphy uses radioactive material, there's a lot of government regulation involved in using the equipment. Thus, most of the scintigraphy units are found in large facilities such as referral hospitals and universities.

When a horse is evaluated by scintigraphy, he is given an injection of a radioactive material in his jugular vein. This material rapidly circulates throughout the horse's body. The horse's legs are then scanned with a camera that measures the amount of radiation in various areas of the horse's legs. If there's an abnormally high amount of radioactivity in a certain spot, that area can be suggested as being the source of the horse's problem.

Scintigraphy relies on the presence of the process of inflammation in helping to determine an area of soreness. When an area of the horse becomes inflamed, blood vessels in the area begin to leak fluid between the cells that make up the vessels themselves. (Incidentally, the leaking of fluid is also one of the reasons why inflamed areas tend to get swollen.) In a "leaky" area of the horse's body, the radioactive material that is shot into the horse will be found in a higher concentration than in the surrounding areas. Thus, if an area of the horse shows a high level of radioactivity, that area is generally considered to be inflamed and it can be inferred to be the source of the horse's problem.

That's the good news. The bad news is that scintigraphy is not a particularly precise diagnostic technique. That is, although you use scintigraphy to help localize the general area of the horse in which a problem occurs, it won't tell you exactly what or where the problem is. Scintigraphy does not allow you to "image" an inflamed area like X rays do. You can't use the technique to see what's going on inside the horse's body. You can only infer that a particular area of the horse, such as the heel, is a problem. It's a useful diagnostic technique for the evaluation of lame horses but not one that is guaranteed to give you an answer to your horse's lameness problem if that problem is suspected to be navicular syndrome.

Response to Therapy

It should be frustratingly obvious that there's no easy way to make a diagnosis of navicular syndrome in a horse. After all your diagnostic efforts in a horse with characteristic lameness and all the typical clinical signs, it still might not be possible to say with any authority exactly what condition your horse has. Therefore, some experts suggest that a diagnosis of navicular syndrome should not be made until a horse fails to respond to any type of therapy for at least three months. Three months should be enough time for most conditions to show at least some improvement with treatment. Unfortunately, most horses with deterioration of the navicular bone don't ever get better.

Making the diagnosis of navicular syndrome in a horse is rarely easy or clear. Unfortunately, many people seem to think that it is. For example, when noticing that a horse is a bit lame, some people will wonder, "Gee, I wonder if he has a touch of navicular?" as if that were the most common cause of lameness in the horse (which it absolutely isn't). That's sort of like wondering if your friend, who's feeling a little under the weather, might have a "touch of cancer."

Even if proper diagnostic procedures are followed, sometimes the diagnosis of navicular syndrome still can be elusive. For example, a horse can be lame, have soreness to hoof testers, go sound after his heels are anesthetized, have some changes on his X rays and still not have navicular syndrome. To further complicate matters, in the author's experience, all of the obvious signs of navicular syndrome discussed above are rarely present in an individual horse. To tell the truth, from a diagnostic standpoint, navicular syndrome is a real pain.

Lameness involving the horse's heels is quite common, probably the most common of all causes of lameness in the horse. Lameness involving the navicular bone is much less so. The current state of diagnostics in veterinary medicine sometimes results in difficulty in separating heel lameness from lameness specifically associated with the navicular bone and its associated structures. However, given the poor prognosis for recovery from "true" navicular syndrome (and the good prognosis for heel soreness getting better), it behooves you and whoever is looking at your horse to approach the diagnostic process carefully and thoughtfully so that you don't make a big mistake. You don't want to unwittingly condemn a horse that, with a little time and treatment, just might get better.

CHAPTER 5

Medical Treatment of Navicular Syndrome

WHATEVER THE METHOD THAT YOU USE TO MAKE IT, once a diagnosis of navicular syndrome has been made, of course you are going to want to try to treat your horse and make him better. You could probably guess that this is rarely an easy condition to treat. As you might expect with a condition that's as complicated and difficult to diagnose as navicular syndrome, there's no sure-fire cure. Still, medical treatment strategies are available to help control the pain of the condition as well as to try to get to one of the possible root causes of the problem. Any or all of them can be tried; none of them may work very well.

NONSTEROIDAL ANTI-INFLAMMATORY DRUGS

Nonsteroidal anti-inflammatory drugs (NSAIDS, for brevity's sake) are among the drugs most commonly used to treat navicular syndrome. Drugs of this class include phenylbutazone ("bute"), flunixin meglumine (Banamine), naproxen and aspirin, among others.

NSAIDS have two primary effects on the horse. The most obviously useful effect is the relief of pain and inflammation. Navicular syndrome causes the horse a big pain in the foot; by giving him a drug that relieves pain, he may be able to use his foot in a more normal fashion. NSAIDS do not "cure" the problem of navicular syndrome. They do, however, help to cover up the pain, allowing the horse to travel in a more normal fashion.

A second, possibly beneficial, effect of these drugs is their effect on the horse's circulation. NSAIDS inhibit the formation of blood clots. This is a result of their effect on a type of blood cell called a "platelet." Platelets are the cells responsible for starting the blood-clotting process. (This anti-clotting effect of NSAIDS is why people who have had heart attacks are sometimes advised to take an aspirin a day. It helps prevent blood clots in the heart.) If you buy into the idea that navicular syndrome is related to problems in the horse's circulation, then giving a drug with some anticoagulant activity makes some sense. There's never been a study done to investigate whether or not the anticoagulant effects of NSAIDS are actually useful in the treatment of navicular syndrome, however.

All these drugs work in a similar fashion along similar chemical pathways, although there are differences in the ways the individual drugs work. There are certainly significant differences between the costs of the various drugs. Some horses do seem to respond better to one drug than another, so it's probably worth it to try another one if the first one that is prescribed doesn't seem to help your horse.

NSAIDS have gotten an unjustified bad reputation in the horse community as being loaded with adverse side effects. Horse owners seem to be especially concerned about side effects on the horse's stomach (gastric ulcers) and kidneys (kidney failure). While it is true that these side effects have been seen in horses given NSAIDS, bad effects are exceedingly rare when recommended doses of the drugs are given. No drug is completely safe 100 percent of the time. However, if you follow the recommended dosage of NSAIDS, it is extremely unlikely that you will ever see a problem in your horse, even if he is maintained on the drugs for years.

STEROIDS (CORTICOSTEROIDS)

The other potent anti-inflammatory compounds given to horses are called steroids. Actually, steroids are a whole group of compounds that have a variety of effects on the horse. Corticosteroids are one group of these chemical compounds. The particular effect of corticosteroids is to strongly inhibit and suppress inflammation. By directly reducing inflammation, they also help indirectly to relieve pain associated with various conditions.

Corticosteroids may be given to a horse orally or by direct injection into an inflamed area. Local injections are the more common method of administration of this type of drug to horses suffering from navicular syndrome. However, corticosteroids do not cure a disease by relieving inflammation. The relief obtained from steroid injections is often only temporary unless the underlying problem can be corrected.

In the treatment of navicular syndrome, two areas of the horse may occasionally be injected:

1. Navicular bursa injections. If there is inflammation of the navicular bursa, it may occasionally be relieved by direct injection of steroids into the bursa. This is a rather tricky procedure, however. It's actually quite difficult to place a needle between the horse's heels and into the horse's navicular bursa (although the procedure for doing so has been described in books and magazines). Direct viewing of the foot with a fluoroscope during the injection

48

process has shown how hard it really is to do right. It's impossible to be 100 percent certain that you are actually in the navicular bursa if you don't attempt to look inside the foot while you are doing the injection. Even if you do get a good navicular bursa injection, studies have shown that the beneficial effects are generally short and temporary.

2. Coffin joint injections. If there is pain and inflammation associated with the coffin joint or the structures associated with it (see chapter 1), direct injection of corticosteroids into the joint may help provide some relief to the horse. Unlike the navicular bursa injection, this injection is not difficult. Frequently, coffin joint injections of corticosteroids are combined with hyaluronic acid (another anti-inflammatory compound that is a component of normal joint fluid), hopefully to help increase the anti-inflammatory effect.

ISOXSUPRINE HYDROCHLORIDE

Isoxsuprine is a drug that causes dilation of the small blood vessels found in the peripheral circulation in people. These small blood vessels exist in the extremities (hands and feet) and in the brain. Small peripheral blood vessels usually carry blood that flows at very low pressure. Since the pressure driving the blood flow is so low, it's likely that the flow can be stopped or slowed down by various medical conditions relatively easily. In people, isoxsuprine is used to try to help dilate these small blood vessels to help relieve the effects of blood insufficiency in the brain and other tissues. Interestingly, the drug is considered as only being "possibly effective" for use in people by the US Food and Drug Administration. That is, the FDA isn't sure if or how well the drug works at doing what it is supposed to do.

In the horse, isoxsuprine was first investigated for the treatment of navicular syndrome around 1980. Its use was considered because of the theories that navicular syndrome is caused by problems with blood circulation to the navicular bone. By using isoxsuprine, it was hoped that any circulation problems in the foot could be relieved by dilating the small blood vessels there. By dilating the blood vessels, the circulation could be theoretically "improved" and the problem would thus take care of itself.

Indeed, two studies have shown that many horses with navicular syndrome do benefit from administration of isoxsuprine. This experimental data is confirmed by the clinical experience of veterinarians as well. Consequently, isoxsuprine is one of the most commonly prescribed drugs for treatment of navicular syndrome in use today. It is curious, however, that no one really seems to know how the drug works. Perhaps if the flow of blood to the navicular bone is "improved," the horse will get better due to a healthier environment being created for the bone. Alternatively, if the flow of blood away from the bone is "improved" with isoxsuprine, perhaps the pressure that builds up in the navicular bone as a result of sluggish blood flow is somehow relieved. Amazingly enough, either way, no one has demonstrated that the circulation to the feet is actually affected by isoxsuprine. In fact, one study that was performed on horses was unable to find the drug in the circulation of the horse after it was given! However, the bottom line is: The drug seems to help many horses.

Importantly, the response to isoxsuprine is not dose dependent. That is, if the prescribed dose of isoxsuprine doesn't work, giving the horse more won't make any difference. The author has seen horses that have been given up to five times the daily recommended dose in hopes that there would be some "extra" effect for a "really bad" case of navicular syndrome. That just doesn't make any medical sense at all. Fortunately, the drug is very safe, so even if the recommended dose of the drug is exceeded, there are unlikely to be any side effects. (The author has seen one horse that had an apparent allergic reaction to the drug. Allergic reactions can happen with any drug, however.)

POLYSULFATED GLYCOSAMINOGLYCAN (ADEQUAN)

If you believe that navicular syndrome is caused by deterioration or degeneration of the navicular bone (a condition much like arthritis of a joint), then it would make some sense to try a drug that is used in the treatment of arthritis. Polysulfated glycosaminoglycan (PSGAG) is a substance that is chemically similar to substances that occur in normal joint cartilage. These substances are called mucopolysaccharides. PSGAG inhibits the function of enzymes that are released during joint inflammation. There may also be some effect from the drug in regard to protecting the deterioration of the joint cartilage, which occurs with arthritis. (The actual extent of that effect is being almost continuously evaluated. The jury is still out on the actual benefits of the drug.)

Anyway, if the cause of navicular syndrome has something to do with an arthritis-like deterioration of the navicular bone, then the use of PSGAG compounds to treat it makes sense. In 1993, a study was presented evaluating the use of intramuscular injections of Adequan (a brand of PSGAG) for the treatment of navicular syndrome. (Adequan is given by injection into the muscle. It is absorbed from the muscle into the bloodstream. It then travels in the circulation to the joints.) Fifteen horses were in the study, of which seven actually received the drug (the study was done "double-blind" so that the results weren't biased). All of the horses had been lame for less than twelve months.

The investigators in this study concluded that administration of PSGAG did improve the lameness signs in the seven horses that received it. The drug was given according to the manufacturer's recommendations (one shot in the muscle every four days for a total of seven doses).

The only real drawback to this method of treatment of navicular syndrome is the expense (Adequan isn't cheap). Of course, no treatment, including this one, works for every single case of anything (that's the way things go in medicine). Still, the use of Adequan intramuscular injections for the treatment of a horse with navicular syndrome is something you can try when other treatments don't seem to help.

There are forms of glycosaminoglycans sold in feed stores that are intended for oral use in the horse. No one knows how well (or if) they work in the treatment of arthritis, much less for the treatment of navicular syndrome.

ANTICOAGULANTS

If you buy into the idea that navicular syndrome is caused by problems with blood circulation to the foot, another form of treatment that might make sense is the use of anticoagulants. In people who have had a heart attack or a stroke caused by blood clots, anticoagulants may be used to help prevent the formation of clots in the future. The idea behind using this sort of drug therapy in horses with navicular syndrome is identical.

The anticoagulant drug that has been most extensively evaluated for treating horses with navicular syndrome is warfarin (yes, it's rat poison). The effectiveness of treatment has been reported at anywhere from 40 to 80 percent. It's easy to give and it's cheap.

Unfortunately, there are many disadvantages to warfarin treatment. Since the drug stops blood from clotting, you have to monitor the horse carefully to make sure he's not getting too much. You have to take blood tests continually to make sure you haven't had too much of an effect on the blood's ability to clot. (You don't want your horse with navicular syndrome being treated with warfarin to bleed to death from a cut.) Also, bleeding in a number of sites such as the chest cavity or abdomen, joints, ovaries or the sheath of male horses (to name just a few; bleeding can be seen almost anywhere) has been seen in warfarin-treated horses. Finally, warfarin interacts with many drugs that are used to treat horses for other conditions, such as phenylbutazone, antihistamines and corti-costeroids. These disadvantages have kept warfarin therapy from being widely used in the treatment of navicular syndrome.

FUTURE DRUG STRATEGIES

Other drugs that affect the blood supply to the horse's foot may also someday be used in the treatment of navicular syndrome. Mentrenperone helps stop blood vessels from spasm and contraction; its effects are supposed to be similar to the effects of isoxsuprine. Pentoxifylline is a drug that allows red blood cells to become more flexible and helps reduce blood clotting, but it hasn't been tried in horses yet. These most likely will be tried in the future.

ACUPUNCTURE

Acupuncture is an ancient form of medicine that theoretically could be of some benefit in treating horses with navicular syndrome. A full discussion of the reported effects and benefits of acupuncture is beyond the scope of this book. Acupuncture has been demonstrated to cause some temporary relief of pain in some animal conditions (but not, so far, pain associated with navicular syndrome). However, it seems unlikely that acupuncture could effect a permanent cure for the condition.

MAGNETIC THERAPY

There's currently a big rush to apply magnets to any part of a horse that hurts. Magnets are supposed to "increase" or "improve" the circulation to injured areas of the horse. Supposedly, better circulation would allow for improved healing.

In fact, no such effect has ever been demonstrated in the horse (or any other species, for that matter). Improvements or increases in circulation have not been shown to be possible in the horse. Nor has improved healing been demonstrated, even if such improvements could be created! However, purveyors of magnetic devices or pads are doing a booming business in supplying something to people in search of a quick and easy solution to a complex and difficult problem. Although there's no demonstrable benefit to the horse from applying magnetic devices for the treatment of navicular disease, they're not likely to hurt anything except your wallet.

REST

Time heals all wounds, supposedly. In many cases this is true. For the treatment of lameness associated with navicular syndrome, time may bring about a cure in some horses as well.

Particularly if you subscribe to the theory that navicular syndrome is caused by some sort of change in the navicular bone in response to stress, some time off to allow for the horse to go through the changes is not a bad idea. In addition, if you are making some changes to the horse's foot in an effort to alter the stress on it, it will take time, possibly as long as six months, for those changes to occur. Apparently, some horses that suffer from navicular syndrome will eventually return to soundness if they are just rested long enough. (Sadly, you can't predict in advance which ones they will be.) And, of course, if your horse has been diagnosed with navicular syndrome and he really doesn't have it (a regrettable possibility that can occur easily enough), chances are, with enough time off, he's going to get better anyway!

EXERCISE

Yes, this treatment is just the opposite of rest. However, you can make an argument that exercise may be beneficial in some horses with navicular syndrome. Exercise has been shown to increase the blood flow to the foot. Exercise also helps to increase the effect of any shoeing treatment. (For example, if you are trying to get the horse's foot to expand with a "corrective" shoe, making him walk on the shoe should help the shoe do its job.) Some horses with navicular syndrome may benefit from exercise, up to thirty minutes a day, after proper shoeing (see the following chapter). However, some horses with sore feet just get more sore if they are worked.

Unfortunately, in some horses with navicular syndrome no amount of therapy is going to return them to soundness. Not only does no one treatment for navicular syndrome work on every horse, some horses won't respond to any treatment at all! If structural changes have taken place in and around the navicular bone as a result of disease, the horse is not going to get better. If, for example, scar tissue has formed between the navicular bone and the overriding deep flexor tendon, no amount of time is going to take away that scar tissue. These poor horses will have a permanent lameness problem to deal with. How to care for these horses becomes part of the philosophy of dealing with a horse that has navicular syndrome (see chapter 8).

CHAPTER 6

Horseshoeing Strategies for the Treatment of Navicular Syndrome

WHATEVER ELSE YOU MIGHT HAVE TO SAY ABOUT navicular syndrome, there's no arguing that the problem affects the horse's foot. And for better or worse, no part of the horse can be manipulated by man as much as the foot. So, inevitably, the foot gets a lot of attention when it comes to the treatment of navicular syndrome. By trimming the foot and applying various shoes, pads and other devices, people make efforts to right the wrongs that they perceive in their horses.

Good foot care and corrective horseshoeing can help a lot of horses with navicular syndrome get better. Unfortunately, there's no single way that's guaranteed to help every horse. Furthermore, some horses can't be helped by any form of shoeing or trimming. Still, it helps to be aware of the many suggested forms of horseshoeing care available for the horse with navicular syndrome so that you can try as many things as possible.

THE NORMAL FOOT

In order to figure out if your horse has any problems in his feet, you should most likely consider what the horse's foot is supposed to look like and how it works. Then, if your horse doesn't fit the "normal" picture, you can take some strides to get him there.

Hoof Angle

If the bottom of the foot is on level ground, the front part of the hoof wall forms an angle with the ground (and the bottom of the foot). For most horses, the angle of the front foot is normally between 50 and 55 degrees. (Some people will tell you that the angle should be lower than this, something on the order of 45 degrees. That's just not right, according to all of the studies that have been done.)

Individual horses can vary within this normal range. There's no "right" angle for every horse (not every person wears the same size shoe, either). Horses can even have a different angle for each foot and still be normal.

The "right" angle for a horse is said by some people to be the same as the angle from the withers to the point of the shoulder. While that may be true, it's not the easiest measurement to make (particularly on, say, a fat horse with no withers). An easier, more commonly used way to see if the horse has the proper hoof angle is to make sure that there is a continuous straight line running from the pastern to the ground. (This angle is most easily seen when the horse is viewed from the side with the horse standing on the foot in question.) This line is called the hoof/pastern axis (figure 7).

Once you can see that the hoof is trimmed so that there is a straight line from the pastern to the ground, you can pick up the hoof and

· FIGURE 7 ·

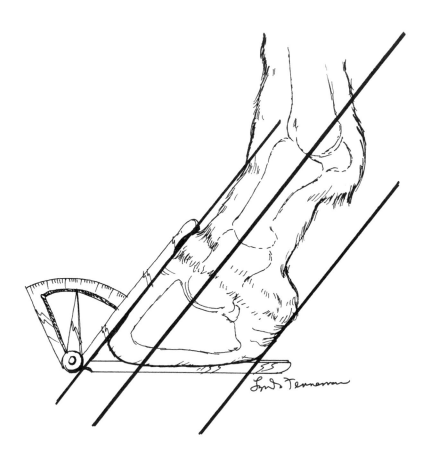

The angle of the foot (measured along the front of the hoof wall) and the hoof-pastern axis (measured down the middle of the pastern, from the fetlock joint to the ground) ideally should be identical.

measure the angle. Gauges are available to do just that. Your farrier should have one. If not, get one yourself. Keep records. (This takes a few minutes.) You want to do all you can to keep problems from occurring in your horse.

Foot Length

The length of the foot is a pretty important subject. There has to be enough foot to cover and protect the sensitive structures underneath the hoof from impact with the ground. If a horse's foot is too short, he's going to feel the same way that you would if you ran around barefoot on the pavement all day. A short foot can get sore and bruised very quickly. Conversely, a foot that is too long may make the horse stumble or trip. The length of the foot is measured from the hair at the coronary band (from where the hoof grows) to the ground at the front of the foot (the toe). It's been done that way since the days of Alexander the Great (really!), so it's a time-honored way of measurement.

Like foot angle, the proper foot length for your horse is a matter of each individual horse. Still, some general guidelines have been developed for foot length:

1. For smaller horses (between 800 and 900 pounds), the toe length should probably never be shorter than three inches.
2. For medium-size horses (between 950 and 1,050 pounds), the toe length should probably never be shorter than $3^1/4$ inches.
3. For larger horses (those over 1,150 pounds), the toe length should probably never be shorter than $3^1/2$ inches.

Make sure you don't overlook the length of the foot when your horse is being evaluated for lameness. The length is an easy measurement to make. If the length of the foot isn't appropriate for your horse, you may end up with some troubles that could get confused with navicular syndrome.

Balance

The balance of the horse's foot describes a relationship between one side of the foot and the other. It's commonly felt that it's important that one side of the foot be the same length as the other side. The top of the foot (at the coronary band) should look parallel to the ground when viewed from the front, and the heels should be the same length when viewed from the side. Finally, when a properly balanced foot is picked up, half of the foot should be on either side of the frog (figure 8). Once a foot is balanced, the foot should land flat (not on one side or the other) when it hits the ground.

Balancing a foot is indeed a noble goal. The true importance of minor imbalances in the hoof is a subject for discussion, however. Studies have shown that by changing the side-to-side balance on the foot, you actually do very little to alter how the stress is applied to it. No matter what the side-to-side balance, the inside heel on the front leg receives the most stress during a stride. Furthermore, as the foot grows, the balance that you started with can change. However, even though its actual importance to the horse can be difficult to assess, a properly balanced foot is still a good thing to shoot for.

Heels

As has been noted, the heels of the horse's foot take quite a pounding. Accordingly, there are some people who feel that the more heel a horse has, the more protection will be given the foot and the better off he will be. To some extent, this is probably true. Horses with low or no heels have been shown to have a variety of ailments associated not only with the foot but with the whole lower leg.

However, more is not necessarily better. While a horse should have an adequate amount of heel, it's important to keep the idea of balance and proper angle in mind, too. A horse can have too high a heel; that's not

· FIGURE 8 ·

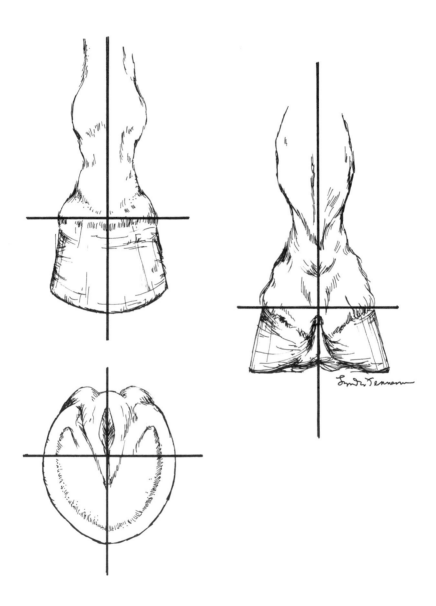

When ideally trimmed, a foot should be symmetrical and balanced when seen from the front, the back and the bottom.

any better than one that is too short. Keeping a horse's heels long is not necessarily a good idea and certainly no way to prevent a horse from developing navicular syndrome.

SHOEING THE HORSE WITH NAVICULAR SYNDROME
Correcting Pre-existing Abnormalities

It goes without saying that proper shoeing and trimming and good hoof care will go a long way towards helping to keep your horse sound. Unfortunately, most horses don't have a perfect "normal" foot. Of course, the feet they come with are the only ones they have, so you just have to make the best of them.

Prior to applying any sort of artificial protective device or shoe to the foot, it's important to trim the foot to make it as close to "normal" as possible. It's generally thought that certain hoof abnormalities are associated with the development of navicular syndrome in a horse. Some of the specific abnormalities include:

1. A broken hoof/pastern axis. The hoof/pastern axis is an imaginary line that can be drawn through the horse's lower leg when the leg is viewed from the side (as discussed earlier). A line drawn through the center of the hoof and pastern intersects with the flat line of the ground and can be seen to make an angle with the ground. This line should be parallel to the normal angle of the hoof. (See figure 9.)

    If the horse's foot is at an improper angle, the normal straight line that should be seen in a properly trimmed foot doesn't exist. Instead, the line bends or breaks at the coronary band of the horse's hoof. If the horse's heels are too high, the line (the axis) will

· FIGURE 9 ·

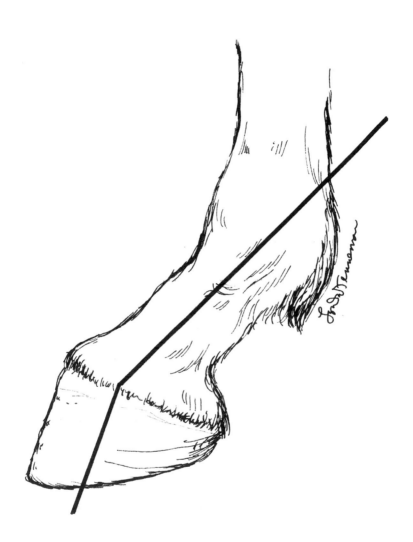

This horse has a broken back hoof/pastern axis.

be broken forward. Conversely, if the heels are too low, the axis will be broken back.

Neither of the above abnormal situations is desirable for the horse. Proper trimming, by raising or lowering either the toe or the heel, helps ensure that the horse has an unbroken hoof/pastern axis. You want to try to make sure that the foot has the proper angle for that particular limb.

2. Underslung (some people use the term "underrun") heels. Research has shown that when a horse strides, he normally lands with the majority of his weight on the heels. A horse with low or underslung heels has little hoof tissue under the back part of the foot to absorb his weight when he moves. If the horse's heel is abnormally low, the sensitive and important structures of the back part of his foot may take an increased pounding. This almost certainly predisposes a horse to developing sore heels. It may also be associated with the development of navicular syndrome. (See figure 10.)

    It's difficult to correct a horse that has underslung heels. Obviously, you can't make a horse grow more heel by cutting on that part of the foot. However, you can help restore some of the normal angle of the foot by working on the horse's toe. Over time, generally many months, it may be possible to help a horse grow some heel by trimming and shoeing. Until such time as the horse does grow some heel, however, frequently some sort of artificial device such as a pad is used to help protect, cushion and raise the heels.

3. Sheared heels. The heels of a horse's hoof are said to be sheared when one of the two heels on that hoof is noticeably higher than the other. In addition, the hoof wall on the higher heel is usually more vertical than normal. The hoof wall on the more normal heel

· FIGURE 10 ·

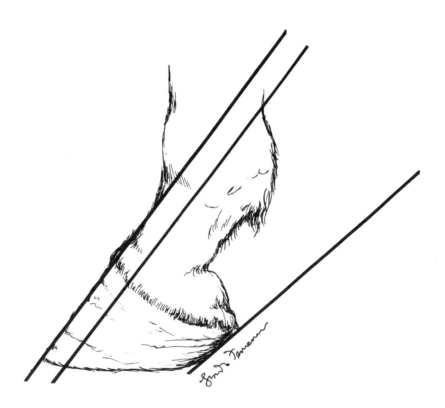

This horse has a mildly underslung heel.

also tends to flare out. (This is most easily seen when the hoof is viewed from behind.) Shearing of the heels can result in heel soreness for the horse. It may also be associated with the development of navicular syndrome. (See figure 11.)

Correcting sheared heels takes some time and can be quite difficult to accomplish. It's not something that can be done in a single trimming. Efforts are made to take pressure off the heel that is too high so that it can drop lower to the ground. Meanwhile, the rest of the foot is balanced and supported with some sort of shoe, such as a bar shoe (discussed later in this chapter).

4. Contracted heels. Contracted heels are heels that are too close together. In fact, the whole foot in a horse with contracted heels can tend to be narrow. Although it's a somewhat subjective assessment, if the heels are too close together, the foot can't expand and contract properly with the normal movement of the horse. If the foot doesn't work properly, it can't properly relieve the stress applied on it. Thus, contracted heels also can lead to chronic heel soreness and, possibly, the development of navicular syndrome.

Correcting contracted heels is also a time-consuming process. In fact, it can be quite difficult to do if the horse is kept in shoes at all! By taking the horse out of shoes altogether, spreading of the foot is encouraged. Some people even go so far as to encourage the horse to stand in water or mud in an effort to soften the feet and help them spread out. (How well this sort of thing works is anyone's guess.) A variety of corrective shoeing methods are also described for the treatment of contracted heels, such as heel springs or "slipped" shoes.

Some horses are born with a foot in which the heels are contracted. Others develop the problem over time, due to improper trimming and shoeing. Horses that develop contracted heels due

· Figure 11 ·

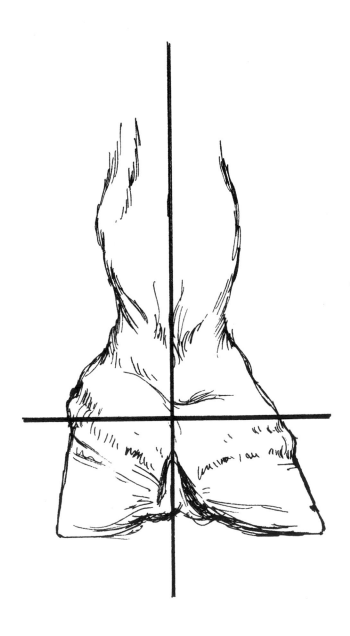

This horse has sheared heels.

to improper trimming and shoeing seem to be easier to return to normal by good hoof management than are horses born with the problem.

5. Small feet (on a big horse). Small feet are not something that can readily be changed. It's theorized that a small foot on a big horse takes more stress than a bigger foot would. More stress presumably increases the likelihood that the horse will develop navicular syndrome.

   About the only thing you can do for this "problem" is to shoe the horse with as large a shoe as possible. (Of course, not all large, small-footed horses will develop navicular syndrome.) You also want to set the shoe wide to allow for maximum expansion of the foot. Then, cross your fingers.

6. Improper trimming and shoeing is a man-made addition to the stresses that are normally placed on a horse's foot. A full discussion of horseshoeing theory is beyond the scope of this book. However, some general rules for proper shoeing and trimming of the horse's foot are:

   a. The trimmed foot should be level from side to side.

   b. The trimmed foot should be balanced from front to back, from side to side and on the bottom.

   c. The trimmed foot should be of an appropriate length and at the proper angle.

   d. The sole should be cupped as much as possible. That is, the sole should be trimmed out so that when weight is placed on the foot, it can expand.

      To demonstrate this effect, put your hand on a counter or tabletop. Make sure that you place it in a relaxed fashion, leaving a small cup in your palm. You can hit the back of your hand surprisingly hard (within reason) with your other hand without causing any pain. This is because the "cup" of your hand flattens and expands and helps to spread out the shock applied to it. The horse's hoof is supposed to work in the same fashion.

e. The heels should be properly supported by extending the heels of the shoes as wide and as far behind the foot as is practical.

f. Nails placed in the foot should not be placed behind the widest part of the foot. This should help to make sure that the foot, especially the heels, can expand.

Pads

The idea behind putting a pad on a horse's foot is disarmingly simple. If the foot hurts, why not put some sort of cushion between it and the shoe to help absorb the shock and protect the foot? Then, hopefully, the horse will move better. In fact, many times pads do help horses with sore feet, even horses whose foot soreness can be traced to navicular syndrome.

Pads are made from any one of a number of materials, including rubber, plastic, leather and numerous synthetic compounds. They come in an endless array of designs, many of them accompanied by various claims as to how their particular style or material makes them especially effective. It's a bit bewildering to try to deal with all the pads and all the claims out there. Clearly, there's no single best pad, or everyone would be using it. Like so many things about navicular syndrome, your best way to approach the question of which pad to use is to try a bunch of them.

Not only does the type of material used to make a pad vary, but the shape of the pad can vary as well. For example, some pads are designed to alter the pressure on various parts of the foot. This effect is especially obvious with pads that have an insert built in to apply pressure to the frog. Applying frog pressure theoretically will increase the amount of weight that the frog has to carry. This can be of benefit to horses with sore heels. In the author's experience, however, frog pressure doesn't seem to help (and occasionally hurts) horses with navicular syndrome.

Wedge pads are one of the most common types of pads used for the treatment of navicular syndrome. A wedge pad is just what it sounds like: a wedge of material that is higher on one end than the other. For the treatment of navicular syndrome, a wedge pad is commonly placed under the horse's heel. This is thought to have several effects:

1. By elevating the heel, it is hoped that strain (tension) on the deep flexor tendon is relieved. Raising the heel would, in theory, relax the deep flexor tendon. (It would tend to straighten out the tendon.) Hopefully, this could help decrease the pressure put on the tendon by the navicular bone as the horse bears weight on his leg.

2. By elevating the heel, some cushion may be provided to the heel area. This would tend to soften the impact in the whole area.

3. By elevating the heel, breakover would be improved.

Breakover is a term that refers to how the horse's foot leaves the ground. For a horse to get his foot off the ground, he must rotate the foot over the toe (breakover) as the leg travels forward. Theoretically, if you elevate the horse's heel, you tend to push him up and forward on his foot. His foot can't sink as low into the ground with a wedge pad on it as it otherwise might. This effect would tend to push him forward and make him break over his toe more quickly. For the horse with navicular syndrome, this might mean that he would stay on his heel for less time and the forward movement of his foot would be made a bit easier.

Investigations have shown that elevating a horse's heel does tend to increase the breakover of the foot. However, it's not a consistent effect. Some horses don't change their breakover when their heels are elevated.

Furthermore, breakover changes are not consistent at all gaits. That is, just because the breakover is faster at the walk doesn't mean that it will be faster at the trot and canter as well.

As a final consideration about wedge pads, remember that in using them, you don't necessarily just want to jack up the horse's heels. You do want to maintain some sort of balance to the foot and a normal hoof/ pastern axis. Therefore, some people recommend that if a wedge pad is used to treat a horse with navicular syndrome, the foot should first be trimmed to the proper angle and then lowered by 3 degrees. A 3-degree wedge pad is then applied to the foot to restore the normal angle and provide the benefits mentioned above. Frankly, although this sort of treatment does seem a bit odd (why not just keep the foot at its normal angle?), it seems to help some horses with navicular syndrome.

Basically, like most everything else about navicular syndrome, you just have to try a pad on your horse's foot and see if it works. If it doesn't, try something else, even another pad. Every change you make is likely to do something. However, you might not be able to predict what that something is. (Understand that you might not be able to find anything that works, either.) Nobody is going to get the right pad the first time, every time.

Corrective Shoes

In addition to the various pads that are used to treat horses with navicular syndrome, a variety of horseshoes intended to correct the problem are prescribed. The variety of shoes that are used seems endless.

Horseshoes were initially devised by the Romans as a method of keeping horses' feet from wearing out. For this purpose, they work very well. In addition to this basic function of horseshoes, an endless array of "corrective" horseshoes have been described as ways to treat and "correct" various conditions of the horse's foot. Farriers are remarkable in their ability to shape iron. The horse's foot often benefits from a creative approach to farriery.

Horseshoes can be something of a double-edged sword, however. While it is true that they protect the foot, they also have the potential for causing harm. Being rigid objects, horseshoes tend to inhibit the natural expansion of the foot. In addition, they tend to concentrate the stress on the foot along the shoe (particularly in the nail holes). As such, they tend to make the wall of the hoof bear more of the weight of the horse than the rest of the foot (normally, all foot structures participate in weight-bearing). Therefore, it's obvious (and very important to realize) that an improperly applied horseshoe may be much worse than no shoe at all.

For the treatment of navicular syndrome, one of several types of horseshoes may be prescribed:

1. Egg bar shoe. A bar shoe is one that places a complete ring of metal underneath the horse's foot. It's closed at the horse's heels by a metal "bar" (as opposed to the "normal" shape of the horseshoe that you would hang over your door for good luck). An egg bar shoe is shaped much as the name would imply, with the "bar" of metal extending well back behind the horse's heels.

   The main way to tell that an egg bar shoe is properly applied is if it can clearly be seen from the widest part of the foot extending back behind the heels. In addition, the bar of the shoe should extend back to the bulbs of the heels (the bulbs are the soft, fleshy part of the heels just below the coronary band). The point to which the bar should extend back can easily be seen when a line is drawn from the bulbs of the heels perpendicularly down to the ground. Egg bar shoes seem to be very useful for the treatment of horses that have underslung heels. (See figure 12.)

· FIGURE 12 ·

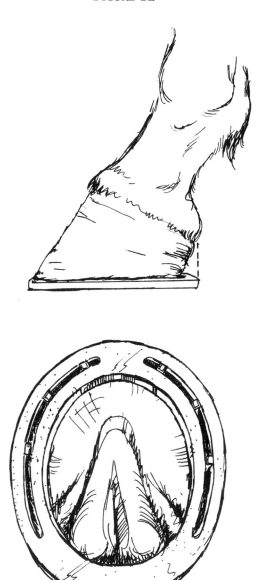

This is a properly fitted and placed egg bar shoe.

2. Rolled toe shoe. If you look at a shod foot from the side, you can see that there is a flat layer of metal nailed onto the bottom of the foot. The thickness of the horseshoe increases the effective length of the horse's foot. This could, in theory at least, help to slow down the breakover.

   In an effort to help the horse with navicular syndrome break over his toe (and get off his heels), some people recommend that the toe of the corrective horseshoe be rolled. For example, the toe of the shoe can be rounded off with a grinder. A shoe with a rounded or rolled toe certainly gives the impression that the horse should be able to roll more easily over the front of it than with a "normal" shoe. As an alternative to rolling the toe, some horseshoes are made from "half-round" steel; that is, in which the metal bar of the shoe is already rounded.

   To increase the effect of rolling the toe, some people recommend an even more dramatic change. By taking off some of the toe with a hoof rasp and bending the toe of the horseshoe up at a slight angle, a "rocker" toe can be made. This may help speed up breakover even more.

3. Slippered heel shoe. In an effort to increase the expansion of the foot, sometimes the heels of the shoe can be "slippered." This means that the back part of the shoe is ground down at an angle, leaving the highest part of the shoe on the inside part of the foot and the lowest part of the shoe on the outside of the foot. Slippering the shoe will, it is hoped, help the foot to expand by causing it, in effect, to slip down the ramp that has been created at the back of the shoe. If a pad is used on the horse's foot, that can be slippered, too. (See figure 13.)

4. Tennessee navicular shoe. This type of colorfully named, premade aluminum shoe has reportedly helped some horses with navicular

· FIGURE 13 ·

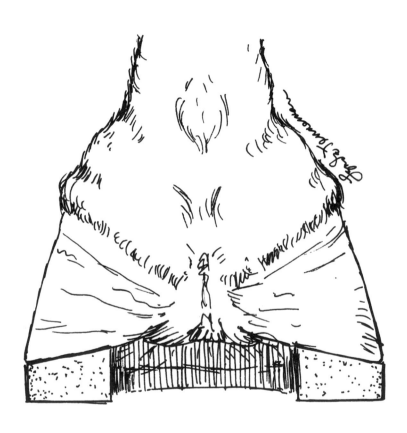

A shoe with slippered heels, such as illustrated here, theoretically will help promote expansion of the heels.

syndrome. It's a type of bar shoe. The shoe elevates the heels due to its deep metal branches, and also protects the heels with a bar of metal.

5. Wide web shoe. These shoes are made out of a piece of metal that is wider than the "normal" horseshoe. It places more metal under the horse's foot, which presumably provides more protection. One advantage of the wide web shoe is that it can easily be set so as to extend beyond the edges of the hoof wall. This is of particular advantage when you are trying to help a horse with a small foot.

Just as with pads, when you are nailing (or even gluing) shoes on a horse's foot, you have to try a bunch of things until you find something that works (if you are lucky enough to find something that works). There are undoubtedly many other types of horseshoes that haven't been mentioned here that can be tried to treat horses with navicular syndrome. Try them if you want to. No one knows something that is going to work every time. You will have to be patient and trust the experience and expertise of the people trying to help your horse with navicular syndrome if you intend to find the best way to shoe him.

SPECIFIC SHOE AND PAD COMBINATIONS THAT HAVE BEEN RECOMMENDED FOR THE TREATMENT OF NAVICULAR SYNDROME

The most successful approach to shoeing a horse with navicular syndrome is to take each horse individually. Each horse is going to respond differently to your treatment (that's one of the really frustrating things about treating horses). Still, you can follow two general rules:

First, you want to try to correct any abnormality of the foot that you can recognize which may be contributing to your horse's problem. This requires some time, care and expertise on the part of your farrier and veterinarian. Make them work together (after all, you're footing the bill).

Second, you want to try to help the normal functions of the foot. You want to do things to help improve weight bearing and absorb the shock and forces placed on the foot. In general, you want to help the foot expand, to support and/or cushion the heels and try to help the horse break over his toe.

Many different ways can be tried to get these things done. Some specific shoe and pad combinations that can be tried to treat a horse with navicular syndrome include:

1. Trim the horse's foot normally. Apply an egg bar shoe.
2. As above, with a pad.
3. As above, with a wide web shoe and/or pad.
4. Trim the horse's foot 3 degrees lower than its correct angle. Raise the heel back up with a 3-degree wedge pad. Apply a shoe, making sure the heels are properly supported and the nails are properly placed (as mentioned earlier in this chapter). Roll the toe of the shoe and slipper the heels.
5. Trim as above. Apply a 3-degree aluminum bar shoe (Tennessee navicular shoe).
6. Raise the heels of the foot to above the normal angle with a pad, and roll the toe of the shoe.

Unfortunately, a lot of finger-pointing goes on in the horse world when it comes to shoeing horses. Everyone seems to have an opinion about the "proper" way to shoe your horse. They are also more than ready to share their opinion with you (whether you ask for it or not). Of course, when your horse has a problem such as navicular syndrome, the chorus of advice only gets louder. People unfortunately have a tendency to start pointing fingers at the person who "must" have caused the problem in the first place.

The best way to deal with all the various conflicting opinions that you are undoubtedly going to receive is to be proactive in caring for your horse's hoof. Get your farrier and your veterinarian working together. Ask your farrier to take measurements of your horse's hoof at each trimming. (Sure, it might take a couple of extra minutes, but it's well worth it and your farrier shouldn't mind if he's interested in doing a good job.) Keep records. Be ready to try various different types of horseshoes and pads; no one knows what is going to work for any given horse. Then, when you get unsolicited and unqualified opinions from friends and neighbors, you can smile and politely nod (maybe even rub your chin in interest), secure in the knowledge that you are doing the best you can.

CHAPTER 7

Surgical Treatment of Navicular Syndrome

In some horses (those that do not respond to any sort of medical treatment or horseshoeing strategy) surgical intervention is the last step. Many veterinarians are reluctant to recommend a surgical solution to navicular syndrome. That's probably for a couple of reasons. First, the decision to do surgery is something of a tacit admission that there's nothing else that can be done. Second, surgery doesn't always work.

Still, surgery is a reasonable option for some horses with navicular syndrome. Of course, once you've decided to do surgery, which surgery do you do? There are several to choose from. In the author's opinion, the ultimate decision as to which surgery to do should be based on the following three things:

1. The likelihood that the surgery will work (and the possibility of side effects).
2. The speed with which you want to the horse return to work.
3. How much the surgery costs.

NEURECTOMY

Without question, the most commonly performed surgery for treatment of navicular syndrome, at least in the United States, is cutting the palmar digital nerves that run to the horse's heels. This is called a neurectomy. It's a surgery that's not particularly difficult to do and one that can even be performed on a standing horse. Many techniques for performing the surgery have been described, including using a surgical laser to cut the nerves. The "best" technique seems to be mostly a matter of the one that the person doing the surgery feels most comfortable with.

A neurectomy is the surgical equivalent of sweeping dirt under the rug. It does nothing to get rid of the problem in the navicular bone area. It only removes the sensation of pain from the horse. It's a quick and easy solution (generally) to the problem. It's a solution that allows many otherwise chronically lame horses to return to normal work. Many horses can return to work in two to four weeks after surgery! Unfortunately, it's a solution that's only temporary because the nerves will ultimately grow back.

Neurectomies seem to generate a lot of controversy in the horse world. Like most things, it's neither as good nor as bad a solution as most people would have you believe. There are a lot of things that people say about neurectomies that fly in the face of reality. Before you can make a reasonable decision about whether or not to perform a neurectomy on your horse, you should know all the facts.

I. A horse will retain some feeling in his foot after a neurectomy. However, he won't be able to feel his heels. He can feel the front part of his foot. He will be able to know where his foot is and how to place his foot precisely and in a coordinated fashion after surgery. He should not be prone to stumbling or other signs of incoordination.

2. The nerves will grow back. After you cut the nerves to the heels, they will try to grow back together (all injured tissue tries to heal itself, even nerves). This can happen as soon as six months after surgery. Even though it's been tried, so far no method of treating the cut nerve ends to stop regrowth of the nerves has been successful. (In 1994, a technique for stopping nerve regrowth by burying the cut ends in a hole drilled in the pastern bone was described. So far, however, this technique has not received general acceptance in the surgical community.)

    Still, you can reasonably hope that your horse will have some good, relatively long-term relief after a neurectomy surgery. According to one study, approximately 57 percent of horses will be pain-free for three years after a neurectomy.

3. There are some complications. As with any surgical procedure, bad things can happen. Complications are not common but you should be aware of them. Complications of neurectomy include:

    Neuroma   As was mentioned above, after a nerve is cut, it tries to heal. While trying to heal themselves, the cut ends of the nerve can grow into an uncoordinated mass of live nerve tissue. This neuroma, as it is called, can be very painful for the horse.

    In an effort to stop neuroma formation, some veterinarians have recommended that horses be maintained on anti-inflammatory drugs for a period of time after surgery (there's no good evidence that this works, however). Sometimes direct injections of anti-inflammatory corti-costeroid compounds can help relieve the pain of a neuroma once it forms. Sometimes, however, another surgery has to be done to cut the neuroma out.

Infection   As with any surgery, there's a risk of infection at the site where you make the incision in the skin. Proper surgical technique makes this complication pretty unlikely.

Infection of the Hoof Wall   You have to keep a close eye on the horse's hoof after a neurectomy. (You should watch your horse's hooves carefully anyway.) Theoretically, it's possible to get an abscess going in the heel, from foot trauma or a nail or the like. The abscess could go unrecognized, since the horse doesn't feel his heel and won't react to what would otherwise be a very painful problem. If you're not paying close attention, a serious infection could develop in the hoof.

Ruptured Deep Flexor Tendon   This complication is quite serious but also rare (fortunately). If there's some sort of a tendon problem in the foot (as opposed to a problem with the navicular bone, for example) and you remove the feeling to the heel, the horse will begin to use his foot normally. Prior to surgery, the horse limped in an effort to keep weight off his injured leg. Normal weight bearing may be too much for an injured tendon. The strain of the horse's full weight can cause a damaged tendon to pull apart. There's not a whole lot that can be done for the horse after that.

Failure to Desensitize the Heels   In some horses, even though they show no lameness after local anesthetic nerve blocks over the nerves to the heel, cutting the nerves does not relieve the lameness. This may be because instead of a single nerve trunk going to the heel, some horses can have little nerve branches off the main nerve. If you fail to recognize and cut these branches during surgery, the procedure won't work. Of course, no horse should be considered for a neurectomy if he doesn't respond to local anesthetic nerve blocks.

OTHER SURGERIES FOR THE TREATMENT OF NAVICULAR SYNDROME

Since the relief obtained from a neurectomy is only temporary, veterinarians have looked for other methods to try to obtain some more permanent relief from the pain of navicular syndrome. Unfortunately, none of them have demonstrated any consistent effectiveness in the treatment of the condition. Even if these surgeries aren't in general use, if somebody brings these things up, at least you'll know what they are.

Suspensory Ligament of the Navicular Bone Desmotomy

In England, a technique for cutting the two suspensory ligaments of the navicular bone has been described as a treatment for navicular syndrome. (In medical terms, cutting a ligament is called a desmotomy.) The idea behind this surgery is that if you cut the suspensory ligaments, tension on the navicular bone somehow may be relieved. After surgery, the horses are returned to work after about three months.

Initially, reports of the success of this surgery were quite encouraging. As many as 70 percent of the horses that received this surgery recovered successfully, according to the initial reports. Subsequently, however, nobody else has been able to come up with the same good results. So far, suspensory ligament desmotomy has not found wide acceptance as a surgical alternative to neurectomy for the treatment of navicular syndrome.

Navicular Bursa Lavage

If you have reason to believe that the navicular bursa is a significant source of inflammation in a particular horse, then treating the bursa makes some sense. Lavage means to rinse something out. Lavage of the navicular bursa is a surgical procedure in which needles are stuck into the bursa so that it can be rinsed out. Any inflammatory by-products would be thereby washed out of the area. If this treatment is going to work, the lameness should improve immediately and one rinse should do the trick. Even though the treatment has been described, nobody has written any reports on the effectiveness of this technique, however.

Inferior Check Ligament Desmotomy

The inferior check ligament is found just below the horse's knee. It is a strap of tissue that attaches the middle part of the deep flexor tendon to the bone behind the horse's knee. It thereby helps to keep the deep digital flexor tendon from stretching too far when the horse bears weight on his leg.

Surgeries to cut this ligament are commonly performed in young horses with an upright foot (called a club foot). By cutting the ligament, the deep flexor tendon is allowed to stretch and relax. This allows the leg to sink into a more normal position. Adult horses with extremely upright hooves have been suggested by some people as having an increased incidence of navicular syndrome. Accordingly, this surgery has been tried in a few cases of that condition in an effort to try to improve the upright conformation.

The surgery and aftercare are pretty straightforward and horses can get back to work in a couple of months. The surgery is assisted by corrective shoeing changes. Like navicular bursa lavage, there are no reports of how well or if this surgery works for the treatment of navicular syndrome.

Fasciotomy

In 1986, some German veterinarians proposed that damage to the palmar digital nerves that supply the navicular area is part of the problem with navicular syndrome. They suggested that if you just relieve pressure and inflammation around the nerves, the condition would improve. Accordingly, a surgery was devised to dissect away any loose subcutaneous tissue or scar tissue from around the nerves (this is called neurolysis). The veterinarians suggested that this technique worked best in horses early in the course of their disease and that had few changes on their X rays.

This is another surgery that hasn't been well studied. Even if it does work, it may be because manipulation of the nerve can cause a temporary loss of nerve function (a sort of short-term neurectomy). It's not a surgery that can really be recommended until more study is done.

As you can see, navicular syndrome is not really a condition for which there is an effective surgical solution. However, for most horses afflicted with chronic pain and lameness, a neurectomy, even with its potential complications, offers the surest bet of the quickest return to normal function, even though that return is only temporary. (Once lameness returns, the surgery can usually be done again.) As with everything else, there just aren't any good simple surgical answers to the complex question that is navicular disease.

CHAPTER 8

The Prognosis and Philosophy of Caring for a Horse with Navicular Syndrome

IT'S A LOT EASIER TO TALK ABOUT WHAT TO DO WITH A horse that has navicular syndrome if you don't own one. It's a lot easier to make dispassionate arguments about what you can do to and for a horse with navicular syndrome if you don't have any emotional attachments to him. Owning a horse is a responsibility. You are the custodian of another being's life. Those decisions are best if they are well thought out and not made in the heat of emotion. In any regard, it helps to know what you and your horse may be in for if your horse actually has navicular syndrome. In the author's opinion, there are three things that you must always keep in mind when dealing with the complex problem that is navicular syndrome.

I. Diagnosis is difficult. In most cases, an accurate diagnosis of navicular syndrome can be time-consuming and difficult to achieve. Your veterinarian may have to make several visits over a period of time to come up with a proper diagnosis. Most afflicted horses will not be so obvious as to have all of the diagnostic signs discussed in chapter 4.

If a diagnosis of navicular syndrome comes easily to someone, be suspicious. Your friends, your horse trainer or even your farrier should not be the ones helping you make a diagnosis. Anyone who looks at a horse and suggests that he has a "touch of navicular" is just being careless. Such a suggestion merely reflects the ignorance of the person making the statement. Diagnosis should be done carefully and thoughtfully.

Finally, realize that since diagnosis of navicular syndrome can be so difficult, some mistakes are going to be made by the people looking at your horse. Some horses are going to be improperly diagnosed. You might find that with a little time and patience, a little treatment and care, your horse may make a complete recovery from some other condition of the back part of the foot that was wrongly labeled navicular syndrome.

2. Treatment can be frustrating and expensive. As you have seen, there are many different strategies for treating horses with navicular syndrome. You may have to explore several different avenues before you find one that works. You may have to wait for several weeks to see if any particular treatment is going to be effective. Or you may not find one that works at all.

The point is, if the first treatment that your veterinarian mentions doesn't work, don't think that he or she is some sort of idiot. Don't assume that because the first therapy doesn't work, your veterinarian and your farrier are incompetent. Let them try any one of a number of things. Get them working together for your horse. Unfortunately, some horses with navicular syndrome don't respond to any treatment.

3. To cut or not to cut? In some horses, surgery may be your last option, albeit an unfortunate one. However, the ultimate question may be, "Do you want to be able to use your horse or not?"

If you are content to have a lame horse, or one that can't be ridden hard without coming up limping, then there's no need for surgery (or any other treatment, for that matter). If you don't mind having a big pet that you can't ride, don't cut on him. Go buy another horse to use however you want.

If, however, you want him to perform at his previous level, surgical intervention, generally in the form of a neurectomy, may be the only way that you can get him there, even if the effects of the operation are only temporary. The surgery is not cruel. However, it is also not a cure. It may be the best that you can do for your horse.

Prepurchase Examinations and the Navicular Bone

Prepurchase examinations are a part of the regular job for most veterinarians who specialize in equine medicine. Understandably, people who are buying a horse want to do whatever they can to make sure that the horse they are buying will be able to do whatever task is intended for him. Nobody wants to buy a horse that has (or is going to have) problems. Consequently, they turn to horse experts to conduct a thorough examination of their prospective horse prior to purchase. The final arbiter of a horse's suitability is generally the veterinarian.

In most prepurchase evaluations, the horse is given a thorough physical examination that concentrates primarily on the state of its legs. The length of time spent evaluating the horse's legs during a prepurchase examination is only natural. Horses are generally pretty healthy. They usually don't have things like heart problems or epilepsy to limit their use. However, they have a multitude of problems affecting their legs. These problems can cause a horse to be unable to do whatever it is that is asked of him. Since horses are used mostly for riding, it's one of the goals of a prepurchase evaluation to try to discover if any of those problems exist in a particular horse. Among other things, veterinarians look for abnormal swellings, areas of pain or surgical scars (that might indicate a previous neurectomy, for example) in an effort to get a clue as to what problems a horse might have.

However, many people don't seem to be happy just knowing what problems a horse might have. They also want to speculate on what problems might lie in the future. Because navicular syndrome is such a problem for horses, they especially want to make sure that their new horse doesn't have it and isn't going to get it. These people want to be able to predict the future. Unfortunately, predicting the future is one thing that can't be done.

There is no way to tell if a particular horse is going to develop navicular syndrome. If he doesn't have it when you buy him (and even that can be hard to tell), you can't tell if he's going to get it in the future. Nevertheless, people still want to try to predict what's going to happen to the horse over time.

During prepurchase evaluations, one of the most commonly requested examinations is a radiographic (X-ray) evaluation of the navicular bone. This is done in a sincere but misguided effort to tell if a horse has, or is going to develop, navicular syndrome in the future. This can't be done. (Please review the section in chapter 4 about navicular bone radiographs. As you remember, it's becoming apparent to most veterinarians that navicular syndrome cannot be diagnosed in a horse just by taking X rays of the navicular bone.)

The author presented a study at the meeting of the American Association of Equine Practitioners in 1994 specifically looking at the significance of X rays of the navicular bone in prepurchase evaluations. The study looked at eighty-five horses and followed the horses for at least one year after they were purchased. All of the horses had navicular bone radiographs taken at the time they were purchased. The navicular bones were "graded" for the degree of the "changes" that were seen in them. The study then tried to see if changes in the navicular bone could be used to predict which of the horses had subsequent lameness problems related to the navicular area.

Three of the eighty-five horses evaluated showed some signs of lameness associated with the heel area of the foot; only one of those three didn't get better on its own. What was the bottom line? It wasn't possible to make any predictions about lameness in a horse's future based solely on the changes in navicular bone X rays. The radiographs were not useful predictors of whether or not a horse would develop navicular syndrome.

So what do you do? Should you take radiographs of your horse's navicular bones prior to purchase? In the author's opinion, there are only two reasons to take radiographs of the navicular bone (or indeed, any area) during a prepurchase evaluation.

One reason for taking radiographs would be if you suspect that a particular area of the horse is a source of soreness for him. If a horse limps on a leg during the examination and your veterinarian can find an area that he or she suspects to be the source of the lameness, radiographs may be a useful way to help determine if there is a problem there. However, a prepurchase examination is not the same thing as a lameness examination. In a prepurchase examination, the veterinarian is usually trying to determine "if," rather than "why," a horse is lame. By taking a few random radiographs, you might not even be examining the area of the horse that hurts! You might not be able to find out why the horse you are considering buying is lame. Most people don't want to do (or pay for) a lameness exam on someone else's horse.

The second reason for taking radiographs during a prepurchase evaluation is to have a record of how the horse looked at the time you bought him. There are a couple of reasons that you might want to do this. For example, you might want to have some sort of record of how the horse looked at the time of purchase so that you can have something to compare to if a problem develops down the line. If the horse is being purchased with the idea that he is to be resold in the future (and hopefully make some money), a set of radiographs, including radiographs of the navicular bone, can be a good selling point and a demonstration of good faith, especially if the horse has never had any problems.

Along the same line, a set of radiographs can be useful insurance in a horse that is intended for resale. Just because you know that navicular bone radiographs are meaningless in a normal horse doesn't mean the next guy will. "Normal" navicular bone radiographs (radiographs that don't show any "changes") generally will not get you into any trouble if you intend to resell your horse. However, you will undoubtedly hear about it if your horse's navicular bone radiographs are somehow deemed to be less than ideal. Only you can assess how much risk you run of not being able to resell your otherwise sound horse if its navicular bone radiographs don't pass someone else's assessment of what's normal.

So how do you sum this up? Navicular bone X rays mean nothing in a horse that's traveling sound at the time he is examined. You can't tell if a horse is going to go lame by looking at its navicular bone radiographs. If you are going to try to predict a horse's lameness future, looking at the radiographs of its navicular bone is just as good as a crystal ball, tea leaves or any other method.

EPILOGUE

THE DIAGNOSIS AND TREATMENT OF NAVICULAR syndrome in the horse is not easy. There appears to be more than one cause of the condition. The diagnostic techniques currently available to the veterinarian are relatively crude and not at all specific to the navicular bone. Because the techniques currently available for diagnosis are not adequate to make an accurate and immediate diagnosis of navicular syndrome, two huge problems occur.

First, many horses that do not have navicular syndrome are diagnosed as having it. This gives the impression that navicular syndrome is a problem that occurs in many more horses than it most likely does. As a result, some horses may be condemned or discarded because of a condition they don't really have.

Second, it's difficult to prescribe an appropriate cure for a condition you can't accurately diagnose. You can't target a specific therapy at a condition if you can't describe the condition. Furthermore, you can't give an accurate prognosis if you don't know how bad things really are inside the foot.

You may have to try many therapies if your horse develops navicular syndrome. Therapies may include any or all of the treatments discussed in the preceding chapters: medicinal, shoeing or surgical. If it ever becomes possible to match a specific therapy to a specific disease process, the success of treatment is likely to improve.

So, knowing all of that, be ready for a frustrating time if your horse does develop navicular syndrome. Consider all your options and do what you think is best, even if it ultimately means that you have to get another horse. As a practicing veterinarian, the author is just as frustrated with the state of diagnosis and treatment of navicular syndrome as you undoubtedly are. We can only hope that future discoveries will make the whole process more satisfying.

BIBLIOGRAPHY

Balch, O. K. et al. "Locomotor Effect of Hoof Angle and Mediolateral Balance of Horses Exercising on a High-Speed Treadmill: Preliminary Results." *Proc. 37th AAEP* (1991): 687–705.

Bowker, R. M., K. K. Wulfen, and D. J. Grentz. "Nonselectivity of Local Anesthetics Injected into the Distal Interphalangeal Joint and the Navicular Bursa." *Proc. 41st AAEP* 41 (1995): 240–42.

Bowker, R. M. et al. "A Silver-Impregnation and Immunocytochemical Study of the Innervation of the Distal Sesamoid Bone and its Suspensory Ligaments in the Horse." *Eq. Vet. J.* 26 (1994): 212–19.

Dyson, S. "Comparison of Responses to Analgesia of the Navicular Bursa and Intra-Articular Analgesia of the Distal Interphalangeal Joint in 102 Horses." *Proc. 41st AAED* 41 (1995): 234–39.

Jackman, B. R. et al. "Palmar Digital Neurectomy in Horses: 57 Cases (1984–1990)." *Vet. Surg.* 22 (1993): 285–88.

Kainer, R. A. "Clinical Anatomy of the Equine Foot." *Vet. Clin. NA Eq. Prac.* 5 (1989): 1–27.

Kaser-Hotz, B., and G. Ueltschi. "Radiographic Appearance of the Navicular Bone in Sound Horses." *Vet. Radiol. and Ultrasound* 33 (1992): 9–17.

Ostblom, L., C. Lund, and F. Melsen. "Navicular Bone Disease: Result of Treatment Using Egg-Bar Shoeing Technique." *Eq. Vet J.* 16 (1894): 203.

Pool, R. R., D. M. Meagher, and S. M. Stover. "Pathophysiology of Navicular Syndrome." *Vet. Clin. NA Eq. Prac.* 5 (1989): 109–29.

Ramey, D. W. "The Navicular Bone and Future Lameness: A Retrospective Study of Prepurchase Examinations in Practice." *Proc. 40th AAEP* (1994).

Rose, R. J. et al. "Studies on Isoxsuprine Hydrochloride for the Treatment of Navicular Disease." *Eq. Vet. J.* 15 (1983): 238.

Steckel, R. R. "The Role of Scintigraphy in Lameness Evaluation." *Vet. Clin. NA Eq. Prac.* 7 (1991): 207–38.

Trotter, G. W. "Therapy for Navicular Disease." *Comp. Cont. Ed.* (Sept. 1991): 1462–66.

Turner, A. S., and C. M. Tucker. "The Evaluation of Isoxsuprine Hydrochloride for the Treatment of Navicular Disease: A Double Blind Study." *Eq. Vet. J.* 21 (1989): 338–41.

Turner, T. A. "Diagnosis and Treatment of Navicular Syndrome in Horses." *Vet. Clin. NA Eq. Prac.* 5 (1989): 131–44.

Turner, T. A. "Navicular Disease." In *Current Practice of Equine Surgery*, edited by N. A. White and J. N. Moore. Philadelphia: J. B. Lippincott, 1990.

Turner, T. A., and C. Stork. "Hoof Abnormalities and Their Relation to Lameness." *Proc. 34th AAEP* (1988): 293–97.

Turner, T. A. et al. "Radiographic Changes in the Navicular Bone of Normal Horses." *Proc. 32nd AAEP* (1987): 309–14.

Wright, I. M. "Navicular Suspensory Desmotomy in the Treatment of Navicular Disease: Technique and Preliminary Results." *Eq. Vet. J.* 18 (1986): 443–46.

INDEX

A

Acupuncture, 53

Adequan. *See* polysulfated
        glycosaminoglycan

Age, of horses with navicular
        syndrome, 27

Anesthetic "blocks," 8, 34–37

Anticoagulant therapy, 52–53

Aspirin, 46, 47

B

Banamine. *See* fluxnixin meglumine

Breakover, 70–71

Breed, of horses with navicular
        syndrome, 27–28

"Bute." *See* phenlybutazone

C

Coffin bone, 2–3

Coffin joint
        anatomy of, 4–5, 11, 13
        anesthetic "block" of,
                36–37
        therapeutic injection of, 49

Conformation, 20, 29

"Corrective" horse shoes,
        71–75

Corticosteroid drugs, 48–49

D

Deep digital flexor tendon, 7, 11,
        12, 36
        rupture of, 82

Degenerative theory of navicular
    syndrome, 22
Digital cushion, 12, 13

E

Egg bar shoe, 72–73, 77
Exercise, as therapy for navicular
    syndrome, 55

F

Fasciotomy, 84–85
Flexion test, 33–34
Flunixin meglumine, 46
Foot. *See also* hoof
    length of normal, 59
    normal movement of, 11–12
Frog pressure test, 33

G

Genetic factors, and navicular
    syndrome, 28

H

Heels, 12–13, 45, 60–62
    anesthetic "block" of,
    35–36
    contracted, 66–68
    sheared, 64–65
    underslung, 64

Hoof
    abnormalities and navicular
    syndrome, 28–29
    angle, 57–59
    balance, 60
    correction of abnormalities of,
    62–69
Hoof testers, 31–32
Horseshoeing, and navicular
    syndrome, 56–78
Hyperextension test, 32

I

Impar ligament, 5, 6, 7, 13, 36
Inferior check ligament
    desmotomy, 84
Ischemic theory of navicular
    syndrome, 18–19
Isoxsuprine hydrochloride, 49–51

L

Ligaments
    definition of, 5
    of the foot and navicular bone,
    5–6

M

Magnetic therapy, 54
Mechanical theory of navicular
    syndrome, 19–22

INDEX

T

Tendon, 7

Tennessee navicular horseshoe,
74–75, 77

U

Unified theory of navicular
syndrome, 22–24

V

Vibrational theory of navicular
syndrome, 21–22

W

Warfarin, 52–53

Wedge pads, 70

Wide web horseshoe, 76

X

X rays
"changes" in navicular bone, 19,
38, 39, 43, 90–92
and prepurchase exams,
90–92